Into the Rising Sun

Vasco da Gama
and the Search for
the Sea Route to the East

Into the Rising Sun

Vasco da Gama and the Search for the Sea Route to the East

Luc Cuyvers

New York

All photographs were taken by the author with the exception of the reproduction on page 2 of a panel from the polyptych *The Adoration of St. Vincent* by Nuno Gonçalves, provided courtesy of the Museu Nacional de Arte Antiga, Lisbon.

Publisher's Cataloging-in-Publication Data

Cuyvers, Luc, 1954–
   Into the rising sun : Vasco da Gama and the search for the sea route to the east / Luc Cuyvers. — 1st. ed.
     p. cm.
   ISBN: 1-57500-064-4

   1. Gama, Vasco da, 1469–1524. 2. Discoveries in geography—Portuguese. 3. Explorers—Portugal—Biography. I. Title.
   G286.G2C89 1998   910'.92 [B]
                                       QBI98-938

The publisher has made every effort to secure permission to reproduce copyrighted material and would like to apologize should there have been any errors or omissions.

Text and jacket design by Joe Gannon.

TV Books, L.L.C.
Publishers serving the television industry.
1619 Broadway, Ninth Floor
New York, NY 10019
www.tvbooks.com

To Alice, Melanie, and Kaye
distinguished producers all,
who'd make any director look good.

Contents

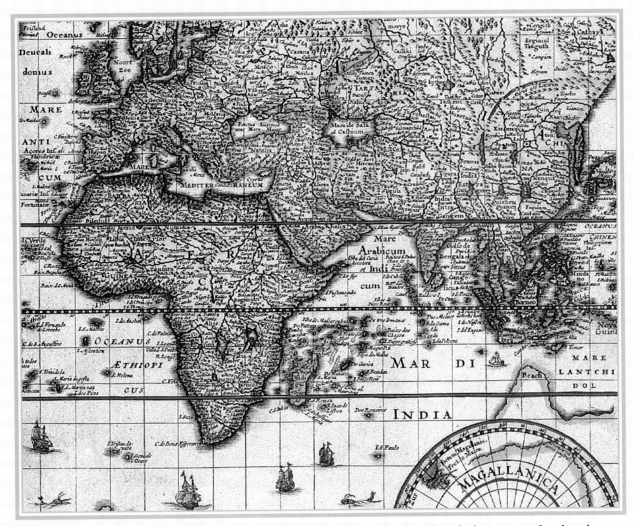

Like Columbus, Vasco da Gama set out in search of the East. But unlike Columbus, he knew precisely where he was heading. For seventy-five years Portugal sent out one ship after another, searching for a sea passage to the Orient.

Acknowledgments

I am often asked why a U.S.-based Belgian would write a book and produce a television series on the Portuguese expansion. I suppose the Introduction sheds a bit of light on the matter, but there is more to it than that. For one thing, there is the issue of my birthplace. Antwerp simply couldn't have reached its position of commercial prominence without the inflow of Portuguese ships, whose owners used the city as their northern entrepôt during the sixteenth century. The Portuguese and their spices brought unparalleled wealth to the city, triggering a golden age of sorts. It lasted until Spain, our mutual nemesis, forced thousands of merchants, artists, and others with different religious beliefs to flee north, giving the Dutch the benefit of a golden age all their own.

This link with my native ground led to some reading and research on the people who initiated the whole thing; men like Henry the Navigator and Vasco da Gama, among many others. Like others interested in the story of Portugal and its search for the Indies, I came away astonished at the speed and magnitude of what happened. That, in turn, was followed by a sense of amazement about the level of ignorance that exists about it. For some reason, people tend to see Columbus as the archetypal Western explorer and the country that sent him out as a race of sailors. This, to put it mildly, is a grave injustice. It was its small neighbor to the west which initiated this entire endeavor and thus deserves the accolades. Coming from a small country myself, just helping to give credit where it is due seemed like a perfectly legitimate reason to pursue the subject.

A few years ago, this interest led to a first film and book in which the Portuguese expansion was included, albeit marginally. It provided an opportunity to visit Portugal and work with its people, and that was the final element needed to put the current project in motion. Portugal is a glorious country, and the Portuguese are a wonderful people. The chance to visit and work with them regularly sealed the deal. From then on I was committed to helping bring the story of the Portuguese expansion and its effects on the shaping of the modern world to a larger public.

Without going so far as to assert that working with the Portuguese is always easy, there is no question that few of my plans could have been realized without their support and consideration. I will always be grateful to Ambassador Fernando Andresen Guimarães and his cultural advisors, Graça Rodrigues and José Sasportes, in Washington, D.C., all of whom took an early interest in the project and followed up by opening doors in Lisbon. There I had the honor of meeting people like Maria João Seixas, then Cultural Advisor to the Prime Minister, António Mega Ferreira, and João Soares Louro of EXPO '98, and Professor António Hespanha of the National Commission for the Commemoration of the Portuguese Discoveries. As a result of their efforts, both the Commission and EXPO '98 later became key sponsors of the project. At the Commission I received considerable guidance from Professor Rosa Perez as well as Jorge Murteira, while Paulo Pinto guided me through the intricacies of Portuguese history. Similarly, EXPO '98's support was extremely well managed by Maria Manuela Furtado, assisted by Alexandra Mauricio.

Initially our plan was to trace the route of the Portuguese explorers by means of the tall ship *Creoula*. This did not materialize for a variety of reasons, but in the meantime I had the pleasure of receiving the support of several people at the Ministry of Defense, including the honorable António Vitorinho, then Minister of Defense, and his Chief of Staff at the Council of Ministers, Jorge Manuel Dias. Also at Defense, Commander Joaquim de Villas-Bôas was untiring in his efforts to keep the voyage on track, prior to his assignment in Brussels. Commander Rui Manuel de Sá Leal, then captain of *Creoula*, and his officers were extremely supportive and generous with their time. I will always remember the informative planning sessions with Lieutenant António Gonçalves in particular. It is a pity we were not able to work on this together, but perhaps we could do so on the Magellan Project. The twenty years or so we have prior to the actual commemoration ought to be sufficient to get the voyage off in time.

Books are usually a fairly individual effort, in contrast to television production. In this case the two interacted, however. In the course of research and production, I had the great pleasure of meeting a number of people who readily contributed their time and expertise, and it is only appropriate that they be acknowledged. So here, in no particular order, is a list of people—historians, archaeologists, sociologists, and many others—who made much of this possible: Dr. Leonardo Cardoso, Ricardo Freitas, Alberto Baeza Herrazti, Dr. José Manuel Garcia, Captain José Malhão Pereira, Amaral Xavier, Pedro Pinto da Silva, Dr. Virgílio Coelho, Dr. João Paulo Costa, Dr. Francisco Contente

Domingues, John Kwaw, Alda Espiritu Santo, Dr. George Abungu, Graham Bellcross, Dr. Inácio Guerreiro, Yourick Houdayer, Dr. K.K. John, Dr. Pratima Kamat, Professor Sanjay Subrahmanyam, Dr. António Sopa, Dr. Cândido Teixeira, Professor Yahya Abu Bakar, Pedro de Almaida, Professor Fok Kai Cheong, Dr. Sunait Chtintarond, Dr. Jorge Flores, Kioko Kojima Kioso, Shin-Ichiro Matsuda, Naoyuki Nakamura, Yasutoyo Samejima, Itaru Takahara, Father Manuel Teixeira, Father Diego Yuuki, Merle Severy, and especially Michael Teague.

Although this is a book, I would also like to acknowledge some of the people involved in the television series it accompanies. Among the early believers were Manuel Petróneo, then the acting head of Radio Televisão Portuguesa's co-production office, who supported the project when it seemed far too early to even think of commemorating the quincentenary of the Vasco da Gama voyage. On the American side, a succession of executives at Maryland Public Television were handed the project, with particular thanks going to Phyllis Geller, Jennifer Lawson, and John Potthast. In Germany, Horst Bennit was an early believer, and it was his vote of confidence that made NDR's participation possible.

Turning briefly to the creative side, Fernando Lourenço, António Escudeiro, Hans Kühle, Colin Taylor, Russ Nichols, Vasco Riobom, and Horácio Henriques were responsible for the stunning photography in the series, whereas João Martinho, José Jerónimo, Alison Nichols, Jason Cowan, and João Diogo handled location sound. My brother Guy wrote a terrific score that greatly enhances all of their work, and arranged it in such a way that it could be recorded by the Belgian National Radio Symphony Orchestra without the production going bankrupt.

As the dedication makes clear, this director was also very fortunate to have Melanie Pefinis, Alice Milheiro, and Kaye Gustafson as producers on the series. The films were shot on what is by current standards a modest budget. If they look far more lush and expensive, it is really as a result of their planning, dedication, and last-minute magic.

Finally, the story of the Portuguese expansion, although fascinating, is not necessarily a major crowd pleaser. Perhaps it has something to do with short attention spans, or perhaps it all seems too long ago to be relevant. Whatever the reasons, our mailbox soon was stuffed with negative replies from organizations that tend to fund this type of thing. But there were some that did support the project, and to them I am very grateful. Aside from the individuals and organizations named above, they include the Luso American Development Foundation, where I was privileged to work with Luís dos Santos Ferro, as well as the Gulbenkian and Orient Foundations. Early corporate support came from TAP–Air Portugal and Ford Lusitana, S.A. There is no way we could have told the story the way we did without their vote of confidence.

To all, a profound thank you. It is one thing to have an idea or a vision. Realizing it takes dedicated professionals, and I am honored to have been able to work with the best.

Introduction

When I was about ten or eleven I received a prize for proper use of the mother tongue at the end of the school year. The teachers handed these things out to encourage us to speak what was known as Civilized Dutch, as opposed to the less civilized Flemish we used among ourselves. Why they picked me is not entirely clear, but at that age one doesn't tend to question these things.

The prize was a big book on the history of the discoveries. On the cover was a massive galleon in an exotic setting, surrounded by South Sea islanders. Inside were magnificent maps and drawings, and though it was a bit unwieldy I used to read it in bed late at night by flashlight. There was something exciting about reading when I was supposed to be asleep. Somehow it added texture. The beam of light dancing over the page brought the pictures to life. Ships appeared to be moving. Soldiers and sailors became real. The people they encountered looked more colorful—sometimes more threatening.

Receiving this book just a year or two after having decided to become an explorer myself, I quickly became familiar with the exploits of Columbus, Cortés, Cartier, Cook, and countless others. But there was one man who intrigued me in particular. Perhaps it had to do something with his name, which sounded like a true explorer. Vasco da Gama . . . It certainly conjured up more exotic images than, say, John Smith. Or perhaps it had something to do with what struck me as an injustice. After all, here was the man who finally reached the Indies, and yet much of the attention went to Columbus, who only *thought* he did. There were maps depicting their travels. Vasco da Gama's extended far into the South Atlantic and around Africa to India; Columbus's trip seemed puny in comparison.

Perhaps it also had something to do with what was going on in those times. While I was reading about these men and their voyages, a new type of explorer was making headlines. The nightly news regularly showed images of astronauts carrying what seemed like suitcases, smiling behind the pane of their helmets and waving, then crawling into tiny capsules. I could almost imagine Vasco da Gama doing something similar—confidently waving to the crowds that lined the docks before heaving his bags aboard. Most people probably thought they'd never see him again, but that didn't bother him. He took off, regardless of the odds.

From that moment I was hooked. Of my own exploratory plans nothing ever came, but I never lost that youthful interest in the discoveries, and especially in the Portuguese part—an epic peopled by men like Gil Eanes, Nuno Tristão, Diogo Cão, Bartolomeu Dias, and Vasco da Gama. Magnificent names of men who searched for a sea route to the East and, in the process, opened the world. Men who deserve recognition, not only because of what they did, but for the world they left in their wake. Which brings us to the reason for this book.

Imagine people five hundred years from now commemorating us. Committees are formed to discuss what to remember and how to do so. What would they pick? And who would be remembered?

Though we can't be certain, it is a safe bet they'll recall our times as the beginning of the digital revolution. They may not associate any particular names with it, but just have a general realization that at the close of the second millennium microprocessors forever changed the ways in which people interacted with one another.

There is also a good chance that they'll remember our era as the onset of space exploration: a time when courageous people in crude contraptions shot themselves in space, made a few orbits, and hoped to make it back. Here they may even recollect a few names: Yuri Gagarin, the first man in space, for instance, or Neil Armstrong, the first man on the moon. And some may recall the leaders who decided to send them there: Nikita Khruschev and John Kennedy.

Historians will emphasize the importance of other events, citing the Cold War or the rise in power of the Pacific Rim, but to most people those will be relatively abstract concepts, dimmed in significance by the passage of time. Instead they are likely to focus on concrete events, like space exploration. We can safely assume that, because it is the sort of thing we remember about what happened five hundred years ago.

While it may take a mental trip into half-forgotten high school history classes, most people have heard of Columbus, Magellan, and Vasco da Gama, recalling them as courageous men who set out to sea in crude contraptions to explore the world. They may also know something about the times and reasons that made them do so: a time of renaissance, rebirth—an intellectual revolution that made people realize that there was more to the world than existed within the narrow confines they had come to know.

What people five hundred years from now may remember about our times is strikingly similar. In both cases one of the key events etched in collective memory is a courageous feat of exploration. In both cases that achievement demanded open minds and a setting that promoted initiative. And, finally, in both cases the names of a few pioneers stand out. Five hundred years ago they were of men like Gil Eanes and Vasco da Gama, sent on their way by leaders like Henry the Navigator and Manuel the Fortunate. Five hundred years from now, they will be of men like Neil Armstrong and Yuri Gagarin, sent on their way by leaders like John the Bold and Nikita the Bald.

This book focuses on what happened five hundred years ago. Some people feel that with the Columbus quincentenary a few years ago just about everything that needed to be said about the discoveries—much of it not very nice—had been said.

If the event was seen as a celebration, that attitude was understandable. Many saw little need to celebrate the death of millions of people and the domination of the survivors by western European powers. But a more compelling case can be made for commemoration than for celebration. Whether we like it or not, what happened five hundred years ago irrevocably changed the world and thus merits reflection.

Columbus also speaks for only one part of the story: the move west, toward the New World. Well before he was even born, the Portuguese were trying to reach his goal—the sea route to the East—by going the "right" way, around Africa. That effort too brought cultures into contact with one another for the first time, shaping the world as we now know it. In that sense the formation of the modern world unfolded on two fronts: one east, the other west. Like the panels of a diptych, the full picture becomes discernible only by looking at both.

Yet for some reason we tend to focus on only one of the panels. Perhaps it is because the move west strikes us as the more exciting of the two. Columbus's voyage was a bold move, a venture that led to a spectacular and totally unexpected result. It still appeals strongly to the imagination. The second panel, though no less exciting, shared little of that impulsiveness. Portugal's explorers searched for the sea route east in a much more organized manner. In fact, their journeys were so well planned that collectively they have been called the first systematic effort at exploration into the unknown.

That is quite a tribute, although we often ignore it. But discussing the Age of Exploration and its implications without mentioning the Portuguese contribution doesn't make sense. One historian compared it to evaluating the space program without crediting NASA, and it is a valid analogy. It was the Portuguese who painstakingly forged the path of the explorers. It was they who developed the technology that enabled a ship to sail to the ends of the world . . . and return. And, in the end, it was they who put their man in India. Columbus promised the moon, but Vasco da Gama delivered it.

The principal reason for going back and reflecting on what happened five hundred years ago is not to unearth clever analogies, however. It is to understand. We live in a complicated world that was forged in the wake of the explorers. It makes sense to revisit that world and to try to see it through the eyes of the people that lived in it. Much in the same way that people five hundred years from now may better understand their times by looking at us, we stand to benefit from reflecting on those who shaped ours.

CHAPTER 1

The Barrier of Fear

This is the story of heroes
who, leaving their native land,
opened a way to the East and further,
across seas no man had ever sailed.

Luís de Camões
The Lusiads, Canto I

omentous events in history sometimes have very inconspicuous beginnings. The Age of Exploration, which so thoroughly altered the map of the world, is a case in point.

For one thing, there is its birthplace—Portugal, a country of, at that time, no more than a million people, isolated along the southwestern corner of Europe.

Why Portugal? Historians often mention a rugged and industrious people, hardened by the weather and the constant pounding of waves along their fragile coast. While this explanation makes for fine prose, it doesn't provide much in the way of insight. True, fifteenth-century Portuguese were probably hardy and tenacious, but there were plenty of others in Europe that would have met those criteria.

Much has also been made of the Portuguese's nautical abilities. A country with hundreds of miles of coast would surely, over time, produce capable sailors and fishermen, but there is little to indicate that Portugal harbored a group of exceptional mariners. Its fishermen ventured out into the Atlantic in small, one-masted vessels, but not farther than others dared to go. Its mariners sailed south from the principal cities of Lisbon and Porto into the Mediterranean and north towards Flanders and England, but like other sensible sailors, they stuck closely to the coast. Though they were capable, there was nothing to set them apart from their colleagues elsewhere.

Cape Espichel, south of Lisbon. Its hundreds of miles of Atlantic coast help explain Portugal's oceanic orientation.

Isolation, too, is often put forth as a defining characteristic of

Fishermen land a catch of sardines in a ritual that has been conducted along Portuguese beaches for hundreds of years.

Portuguese initiative. It is true that Portugal, then as now, was neither politically nor geographically in the mainstream of European affairs, but the point could be made that isolation should have hampered rather than promoted the massive oceanic undertaking Portugal initiated. And if isolation were so important, again there were plenty of places in Europe that qualified.

There are, in other words, plenty of reasons why Portugal shouldn't have done what it did. It was a relatively backward country, with few resources and little wealth. Though it set its present boundaries as early as the thirteenth century, it certainly didn't rank among great powers like France, England, and the Holy Roman Empire, or among economic powerhouses like the small republics of Genoa and Venice. There was little to presage momentous events or even a great future. After all, the country was struggling to simply survive.

In short, without the benefit of hindsight one would be unlikely to pick Portugal as the birthplace of the European expansion. The Portuguese of that time would probably have been unlikely to do so either, for the simple reason that they had no clue what they had started when they embarked. Instead, a combination of people and circumstances played itself out in an isolated corner of Europe and eventually took on a course all its own.

Of course, it needed something to set it all in motion. Which brings us to our inconspicuous beginning.

The year was 1411 and a long string of wars with the kingdom of Castile, Portugal's eastern neighbor, had finally come to an end. For the first time in many years, the country's outlook seemed relatively secure.

Portugal was ruled by King John I, who had soundly defeated the armies of Castile on several occasions. He was popular, especially among the merchants of Lisbon, who controlled most of the country's wealth. "Both the virtues required of a king—justice and piety—were combined in his person," wrote his court historian.

John was married to Philippa, daughter of John of Gaunt, the duke of Lancaster. The marriage strengthened Anglo-Portuguese ties and was, from all accounts, a happy one. A chronicler described Philippa as "sincere" and "friendly to all honest people," diplomatically leaving out that she was determined to get her own way—at any cost—and did so most of the time. She and John had six children: Edward, Pedro, Henry, Isabel, John, and Ferdinand. Luís de Camões, Portugal's greatest poet, would later call them the "Noble Generation," for it was they—especially the three oldest sons—who launched Portugal's astonishing oceanic exploits.

The statue of John I, founder of Portugal's Aviz dynasty, still stands prominently on a Lisbon square.

But in the years following the peace with Castile, oceanic exploration was far from the minds of Edward, Pedro, and Henry. Young, ambitious, and solidly imbued with chivalric ideals, they were eager to prove their manhood, preferably on the battlefield. Since there was no longer any glory to be reaped by killing Castilians, their father suggested a jousting tournament—a major international affair that would serve both as a celebration of the end of the war and an opportunity for his sons to match their skills against other knights. The three princes had different ideas, however. Jousting tournaments, while exciting, hardly compared with the honor of battle, so they eagerly supported a secret plan to attack the Moorish port of Ceuta, directly across the Strait of Gibraltar—an operation that would undoubtedly allow for some battlefield heroics. As one of the terminals of the African gold trade, Ceuta was known to be a rich place, so there also was a good chance for some spoils. And, like all of North Africa, the city was in Muslim hands. Here was an opportunity to do battle with the despised infidel, which appealed strongly to their religious convictions. As far as the princes were concerned, any tournament, no matter how prestigious, paled in comparison to the chance of wresting a vital port from the Moors.

King John looked at the plan more dispassionately. The idea appealed to him, but it clearly wasn't without risk. And attacking Ceuta was likely to be expensive, requiring not only an invasion force but also a fleet to carry it there. Then there were others to consider: the Castilians, for instance, who might have similar designs, as might the Genoans and Venetians. On the other hand, whoever controlled Ceuta controlled shipping in and out of the Mediterranean. That could prove very useful. Portuguese ships would be able to seek shelter from North African pirates, and Ceuta could even become a base from which to prey in turn on Arab shipping.

The king examined both sides carefully and then, encouraged by his wife and sons, decided to go ahead. After all, the plan provided dual incentives. There was no question that Ceuta's fall would deal the Moors a major setback, a deeply rooted religious motivation. Furthermore, if the city was caught unaware, there was a rich treasure to be looted, a financial motivation. His council enthusiastically concurred. Even Nun' Álvares, a friend and comrade in arms known for his clearheaded advice, was all in favor. "It appears to me that this plan was not conceived by you nor by anyone in this world," he is reported to have said, "but was inspired by God." Álvares's endorsement was decisive. Preparations for the Enterprise of Ceuta, as it had become known, could now begin in earnest.

Throughout much of 1414 and early 1415, both Lisbon and Porto were busy preparing for the attack. Shipyards along the Tagus and Douro rivers turned out scores of ships, and an invasion army of sorts was assembled and trained.

These warlike preparations were bound to raise suspicions, so the court leaked information implying that they were aimed at the Duke of Holland. At the same time, an ambassador was sent north to reassure the duke that it was no more than a pretense, designed to conceal their real intentions. Combined with strict orders to keep their true objective a secret, the strategy worked. As far as anyone could tell, no one in Ceuta seemed the least bit concerned.

By the summer of 1415, everything was ready. On July 10, Prince Henry, who had organized a contingent of men and ships in Porto, arrived in Lisbon. His seventy ships, gaily decorated with flags and banners, anchored off the city's main square, ready to join a fleet from the capital. But there was a delay. The plague had struck the city and claimed victims among the Court. Henry was informed that the queen was desperately ill, so he hurried to the palace to join his brothers at her bedside. It was the last time he saw his mother. On July 19, Philippa of Lancaster died. With her final breath, she beseeched her sons to go out and gain honor and glory in the conquest of Ceuta.

Along with the deaths of thousands of others, the queen's passing cast a dark mood over Lisbon, and for some time it appeared the Enterprise of Ceuta would be called off. The king was stricken with grief and in no mood to oversee the final preparations. Others saw the ravaging disease as a bad omen, suggesting the plan should be shelved for a later time.

But the princes were not about to give up. Young Henry in particular insisted that the expedition go forward, reminding his father that it was the queen's dying wish that Ceuta be captured for Christianity.

Though his mother's passing affected him deeply, he knew a delay would prove fatal. There was no way the fleet and army could be kept waiting, nor could its destination forever be kept secret. It was either now or never.

The king relented, and on July 23 the combined fleet, the largest ever assembled in Portugal, set sail. Numbering some two hundred vessels manned by nearly twenty thousand soldiers and sailors, it rapidly progressed beyond Cape St. Vincent at the southwestern corner of Europe and headed for the Strait of Gibraltar. But then the winds died, becalming the ships near the village of Lagos for more than a week. When they finally picked up, they were more than the fleet could handle. Just before it reached Ceuta a storm struck, forcing many of the ships back to Europe. Some critics began to murmur that the storm was another bad omen and that the whole thing should be called off, but the princes never wavered. On August 20, four weeks after leaving Lisbon, their force finally arrived at its destination.

One wonders why the people of Ceuta failed to take steps to strengthen the city's defenses. Perhaps they assumed that the Portuguese had given up on their assault after being dispersed by the storm, but it proved a major miscalculation. The city fell in just one day. As soon as its walls were scaled, the Portuguese plunged into the maze of streets and alleys, killing everyone in sight. The young princes led the way, intent on fulfilling their mother's dying wish.

The cathedral at Ceuta. Built on the site of the city's mosque, it still contains reminders of the Portuguese conquest of the city in 1415.

By evening Ceuta was firmly under Portuguese control. Hundreds of its citizens had been massacred, against a mere eight Portuguese deaths. With fewer losses than expected, a thanksgiving mass was celebrated in the city's bloodstained mosque. John took the occasion to knight his sons. After all, that was what they had come for and, according to the chroniclers, they richly deserved it. All three—Edward, Pedro and especially Henry—had fought bravely.

A few days later the Portuguese fleet returned to Lisbon. News of the conquest had preceded it, and the city gave the conquerors a tumultuous welcome. Many people couldn't believe their eyes. Just a few years earlier the constant threat of war with Castile had cast a pessimistic mood over the city. Now not only was there peace, but

Portugal had actually gone out and taken some territory from the Moors. No one had done that: not France, not England, not Burgundy—none of the great powers of the time, even by combining their armies.

The news of Ceuta's fall spread quickly through Europe, gaining John and Portugal a good deal of prestige. Yet for all this newly won respect, Ceuta's conquest was not a financial success. For one thing, in their haste to loot the city the Portuguese had put priceless stores of silks and spices to the torch, leaving little to take back to Portugal. For another, a garrison had to be left to guard the city. Three thousand men strong, it depleted the king's resources with little, if any, chance of restoring them. The Enterprise of Ceuta, in short, became a massive financial drain. But no one wanted to admit that. After all, the princes had been knighted and Portugal's restless nobility had been suitably occupied. Moreover, Christianity had gained some ground on the hated Moors. It wasn't much as territory goes, but size wasn't what mattered here.

After the city's conquest, Ceuta was fortified to withstand Muslim sieges. Although Ceuta gained Portugal a good deal of prestige, its defense was a serious drain on the treasury.

It could have been left at that, with the Portuguese tenaciously holding onto their North African base, secure in the knowledge that they had made the first successful attack against Islam in North Africa. That would have been sufficient to earn Ceuta a small place in history, but it grew into something much larger—something none of its conquerors could have anticipated.

About thirty years later, Portuguese chronicler Gomes Eanes de Azurara was asked to write an account of the taking of the city. Like most official histories of that time, it provided a victor's perspective, praising heaven and earth for the victory and emphasizing its importance. Azurara didn't need time to let the story work itself up. As a paid chronicler, commissioned by the court, tales of heroism came to him naturally, with the Portuguese coming across as valiant defenders of the "true faith."

Beneath his heavy-handed prose, however, lie some vital insights. Though Azurara wasn't present during the conquest, he interviewed some participants, which enabled him to provide a reliable account of the plan and the preparations for the attack. More importantly, he shed some light on what would compel the Portuguese to move on, describing in vivid detail the astonishment of the conquerors at the wealth of Ceuta. They saw mansions, built of stone with elaborately carved woodwork, that reflected an affluence most Portuguese could only imagine. Inside were luxuries they couldn't even have dreamed off. Much of this wealth went up in flames, but not before making a deep impression on Ceuta's new rulers.

Combined with the religious fervor that fueled the operation in the first place, that wealth, just across the Strait of Gibraltar, proved irresistible. Back in Portugal most people knew little but deprivation, with many barely eking out a living. Most people had heard of the fabulous riches of the Arab trading empire, but they had always seemed unreachable. Ceuta demonstrated that they were tantalizingly close and could be taken. It also suggested that there was a great deal more within reach. And finally, Ceuta made clear that going after this wealth was a Christian duty and thus perfectly legitimate. God and greed worked in perfect harmony. Together they made the perfect motive to move on.

The Panel do Infante *from a set of panels attributed to Nuno Gonçalves. Shown to the right of St. Vincent, Portugal's patron saint, is Henry the Navigator, his hands folded in prayer. (Museu Nacional de Arte Antiga, Lisbon)*

After completing the story of the conquest of Ceuta, Azurara was commissioned to write another chronicle, this one about the Portuguese expansion. By that time, Portuguese sailors had advanced far beyond Ceuta along the Northwest African coast, allowing him to place the taking of the city in context. And he left no doubt about its significance. "Where could this chapter begin better than in speaking of that most glorious conquest of the great city of Ceuta, of which famous victory the heavens felt the glory and the earth the benefit?" Azurara wrote in the first substantial chapter of the chronicle.

When he wrote these words, Azurara had no idea where Portugal's adventures along the African coast would end, but he could pinpoint their origins. In his mind there was no doubt that the conquest of Ceuta was the curtain-raiser to a much grander drama. But there was a need for something more: a person, or a group of persons, to enable subsequent events to take place, even if by default rather than design.

Azurara addressed that part of the story as well,

although his account is a bit one-sided, giving most of the credit to Prince Henry. It now is clear that Edward and Pedro, Henry's older brothers, also played active roles in the early phases of the Portuguese discoveries, but Azurara hardly mentions them. It was understandable: Edward and Pedro were dead by that time and, for a variety of reasons, had been dishonored. Azurara wasn't likely to delve deeply into their contributions.

Despite these shortcomings, Azurara is our main contemporary source on the first phase of Portugal's maritime expansion, as he has been for every historian who has tried to make sense of that era. Given his proximity to the action, most accepted what he had to say, though some felt compelled to add a few thoughts of their own. Portuguese historians of the sixteenth and seventeenth centuries in particular were fond of adding personal insights. Though none could have known Henry in person, it didn't prevent one from granting the prince a brilliant scientific mind, another from praising his artistic and managerial skills, and still others from emphasizing his prowess on the battlefield.

The monument to the discoveries along Lisbon's waterfront. In front of Portugal's most famous discoverers is Henry the Navigator, who initiated the country's oceanic exploits.

What emerged was a near-mythical figure who led Portugal out of obscurity into the limelight, much the way he is shown on Lisbon's Monument to the Discoveries. Unfortunately, speculation after the fact not only creates false impressions, it also makes things unnecessarily complicated. The Henry depicted in much of the historical record is a psychoanalyst's dream: brilliant, complicated, shrewd, tortured, and given to mystic spells. While there may have been a bit of all of that in him, it doesn't tell us what drove the young prince to set out into southern seas.

It is better to turn to the original source. Early in his second chronicle, Azurara lists the reasons that compelled Henry to look south. Not only are the reasons relatively straightforward, it is possible to separate wishful thinking from reality. Most importantly, here we have someone who knew the prince personally telling us what motivated him. There simply is nothing quite like it.

Henry, Azurara explains, looked south first and foremost because "he had a wish to know the land that lay beyond the Canary Islands."

The young prince, in short, was curious; he wanted to know what lay beyond the imaginary line that separated myth from reality. Around the time of the conquest of Ceuta, that line was drawn south of the Canary Islands near Cape Bojador, in today's Western Sahara. Beyond it, so the general thinking went, the torrid heat of the sun made the water boil, making life, not to mention a course through it, impossible. Others believed that if it weren't the sun, adverse winds or currents prevented passage, along with a set of vicious sea monsters that guarded entry to the void beyond.

As if to confirm these wild speculations, there were stories of those who *had* sailed beyond, never to return. In 1291, for instance, two brothers from Genoa had set sail for the waters beyond Bojador. They were never seen again. Those who had tried to follow in their wake invariably turned back before Cape Bojador, claiming they could see the water boiling or fearing that the swift currents beyond the cape would trap them forever.

Apparently Henry didn't swallow these stories. Along with his brothers, he had received a solid education at a time when Europe was rediscovering classical authors. Their works told of people sailing far beyond the Canary Islands and even circumnavigating the entire African continent. None mentioned great heat, unpassable currents, or sea monsters. Instead, they spoke of successful sea voyages completed thousands of years earlier. For Henry and his brothers that was proof that there were lands beyond Bojador. And they wanted to know what they looked like.

At a time when dogma prevailed, such curiosity was novel and, some would say, dangerous. But Henry, according to Azurara, tempered it with some old-fashioned incentives. "The second reason," the chronicler continued, "was that if there chanced to be in those lands some havens into which it would be possible to sail without peril, many kinds of merchandise might be brought into this realm, which would find a ready market because no other people of these parts traded with them; and also the products of this realm might be taken there, which traffic would bring great profit to our countrymen."

In Henry's view, in other words, there was money to be made. Since no one knew the people beyond Cape Bojador, they might be interested in Portuguese products, he reasoned. More importantly, they might have something Portugal wanted in return. And Henry knew exactly what it was. In Ceuta he had learned of the principal source of the city's wealth: the gold trade with places like Timbuktu and the kingdom of Mali, far to the south. Europe was perpetually short of gold and getting to one of its sources without Arab middle-men was bound to be immensely profitable. But going there by land, through Arab-held territory, was out of the question. The only way to get there, it seemed, was by sea.

With the third reason Azurara entered religious territory. A devout Christian, Henry harbored a tangible hatred towards the Moors and a desire to defeat them on every front. But the prince realized it was essential to know the enemy. Going south, he figured, might help him do so. For that reason, "the said Lord Infant exerted himself to cause this to be fully discovered, and to make it known determinately, how far the power of those infidels extended," as Azurara put it.

Closely tied to that sort of intelligence gathering was the fourth reason. There had long been talk in Europe of Prester John, a mysterious Christian king who reigned over a large part of Africa. Henry wanted to find him, hoping that he and his allies "would aid him in the war against the enemies of the faith." It made eminent sense. Confronting the power of the Moors in Africa with Portugal's meager resources would prove difficult, if not impossible. Teaming up with another Christian power, preferably one that could open a second front, gave the country a chance.

Religion also figured prominently in Azurara's fifth reason: "the salvation of lost souls." Henry didn't expect to convert any Moors, but there was a chance the Portuguese would encounter other people, unaffected by the reach of Islam. If so, he wanted to make sure that they would be brought onto "the true path," reasoning that this was not only his Christian duty but could yield additional allies in the struggle against the infidel.

Finally, there was a reason which, as Azurara delicately put it, "would seem to be the root from which all the others proceeded." He was referring to "the inclination of the heavenly wheels"—Henry's horoscope, in other words. Because the prince's ascendant was Aries, which was in the house of Mars, and because Mars was in Aquarius, which was in the house of Saturn, "this Lord should toil at high and mighty conquests, especially in seeking out things that were hidden from other men," Azurara explained. Henry, in other words, didn't control his destiny. It had been preordained for him.

It is interesting that historians have scrutinized every facet of Henry's life to figure out his motivations when Azurara left us such an elegant list. Since the court paid Azurara's salary, he naturally tended to err on the side of reverence, but there is no reason to dismiss his work as long as we accept that the list was compiled with the benefit of hindsight. It is doubtful, for instance, that at age twenty Henry was thinking of strategic alliances with mysterious African rulers, but that doesn't really matter. Henry's true motivations—profit, religion, and curiosity—are what count, and they shine through clearly.

Profit was something everyone could understand. Putting it high on the list not only proved Henry to be a shrewd businessman but also provided justification for heading into the unknown. The possibility of making money compelled even the most conservative merchant to look less skeptically at the venture. Henry knew that, as long as there was a reasonably good chance of returns, people would be willing to accept the risks.

The desire to convert unbelievers came from the prince's Christian upbringing, and there is no question that his beliefs came from the heart. They too justified the effort. By giving them such a prominent role, Henry imparted that the journey south in search of unbelievers was nothing less than a Christian's duty to God. Who could argue with that?

Finally, there was curiosity—the desire to know what lay beyond—gracing the top of the list. What a wonderfully human motive! Because of his role in the early stages of the discoveries, the prince later became known as Henry the Navigator, but it would have been equally apt to call him Henry the Curious. Everything else was mere justification, though designed cleverly so it could appeal to all.

Some of the motivations were firmly rooted in the spirit of the Middle Ages. The desire to defeat the Moors or turn unbelievers onto the "true path" was not only based on Christian ideals, it was also derived from deeply held chivalric motives. Other reasons were more modern: the desire to make money, for instance, or the obsession to go beyond what medieval chroniclers had classified as the end of the world. Their inclusion reveals Henry as a transitional figure, with one foot firmly planted in the Middle Ages and the other in modern times. It probably took such a man and mind to succeed in what followed.

We can assume that Henry's older brothers shared some, if not all, of his interests. Pedro in particular was a bright man who traveled widely over Europe and is known to have bought many reference works for the royal library. From these he gathered information about the formidable strength of Islam throughout North Africa and the Middle East, convincing him that a frontal attack would be suicidal. Accordingly, he felt the need to outflank the Muslim world by venturing around it, an opinion he shared with his brothers on several occasions.

As first in line to the throne, Edward was forced to focus on different matters, though he, too, was keenly interested in learning. In fact, he spent far more time reading and studying the works of classical authors than preparing for a future reign. There was some concern about this at court, but John I was still firmly in charge. Though already in his sixties, he was strong and healthy. The succession, as a result, wasn't considered a pressing issue.

No one knows when or where the subject came up, but it appears that in the years following the conquest of Ceuta the three princes discussed the possibility of finding a sea route to Africa's gold. They assumed it could be done, but the only way to find out for certain was by heading out into the expanse of the Atlantic. As newly appointed administrator of the Order of Christ, Henry had some resources at his disposal, which probably financed the first few attempts. We don't know whether either of his brothers provided financial support, but they gave their blessings. As they were higher in the royal hierarchy, that was also important.

In 1419 or 1420, the first ship was dispatched, probably from Lagos, along Portugal's Algarve coast, where Henry spent a good deal of his time. Though significant in hindsight, we don't know who captained this first attempt, other than that he was most likely someone from Henry's own household. The crew was probably picked from the Algarve's fishermen and, possibly, merchant sailors. Like their colleagues in the rest of Europe, they were a tough breed but superstitious. To them, the line that separated the known from the unknown was very real. Most felt it wasn't their business to cross it.

With a captain who probably shared these feelings, the early going was tough. Azurara recounted:

> So the Infant, moved by these reasons, began to make ready his ships and his people. But this much you may learn that, although he sent out many times, there was not one who dared to pass Cape Bojador and learn about the land beyond it, as the Infant wished. And to say the truth, this was not from cowardice or want of good will, but from the novelty of the thing and the wide-spread rumor about this Cape, that had been cherished by mariners from generation to generation.

How are we, men said, to pass the bounds that our fathers established, or what profit can result to the Infant from the perdition of our souls as well as of our bodies? We shall become willful murderers of ourselves.

Seeing no hope of honor or profit, they left off the attempt. For, said the mariners, this much is clear, that beyond this cape there is no race of men nor place of inhabitants; nor is the land less sandy than the desert of Libya, where there is no water, no tree, no green herb—and the sea is so shallow that a whole league from land it is only a fathom deep, while the currents are so terrible that no ship having once passed the cape will ever be able to return.

Even so, not all of this time was wasted on elaborate excuses. Rather than risking their lives in unknown waters, some of Henry's captains turned to raiding Arab merchants, returning "not wholly without honor," as Azurara put it. The booty taken from these infidels came in handy, for it enabled Henry to continue financing the voyages without having to dip again into the coffers of the Order of Christ.

More importantly, during the early 1420s João Gonçalves Zarco and Tristão Vaz—two of Henry's captains—sailed west rather than south, and ran into a small uninhabited island. Since it had a fine natural harbor, they called it Porto Santo. The men went ashore and observed that the land, though treeless, appeared fertile. They reported the discovery to Henry adding a recommendation to settle it.

The prince concurred and sent Zarco and Vaz back, along with a group of settlers. Unfortunately, one of them brought along a pregnant rabbit, which littered on the trip to Porto Santo. They set the little rabbits free upon their arrival, which proved to be a big mistake. The animals, Azurara wrote, "in a very short time multiplied so much as to overspread the land, so that our men could sow nothing that was not destroyed by them. And it is a marvel how they found in the following year that although they killed a very great quantity of these rabbits, there yet remained no lack of them."

The statue of João Gonçalves Zarco, one of Madeira's discoverers, stands prominently in the heart of Funchal, capital of the island.

How much of this is true is difficult to say, although it is clear that by then the settlers had learned of another island somewhat further south. They headed there instead. Unlike Porto Santo, this island was

Madeira proved a spectacular discovery. The island was settled in 1425, providing Portugal valuable colonization experience.

covered with an abundance of trees, so they called it Madeira, Portuguese for "wood." There also was plenty of fresh water, making it a perfect place for a new settlement. But here, too, the settlers made mistakes. Early in their stay, for instance, they decided to burn out an area of bush rather than clear it by hand. Before they knew it, the fire raged out of control, destroying everything they had built and planted. At the height of the fire, the colonists even had to seek safety in the sea, going in up to their necks. But once the area had cooled off they started over and, as Azurara observed, "they began to make very great sowings, from the which they obtained most abundant crops."

The colonization of Madeira proved to be an important move. Before long the colonists began to send timber, sugar and wine back to Portugal, which made them, and Henry, a good deal of money. Madeira would also become a convenient provisioning port, especially useful for ships in need of repairs and fresh water. But perhaps most important, it provided Portugal colonization experience, which would prove very useful in the years ahead.

By the early 1430s, the Portuguese had also discovered and claimed the islands of the Azores, but little progress had been made on what interested Henry most: the sea route south, past Cape Bojador, to Africa's gold. Though twelve or thirteen voyages had been sent that way, the prince's sailors invariably lost their nerve near the Canary Islands. Some sailed beyond and got within sight of the Cape, but then they, too, returned.

Perhaps it was understandable. Not only did contemporary chroniclers predict horrible things to anyone passing beyond, Henry's sailors noticed that they were, in fact, entering unpleasant waters. Usually a reassuring sight, the coast was desolate, even sinister. There were frequent fogs, and sometimes winds from the desert covered the ships with a fine, reddish dust. Shallow and tricky to navigate, the waters didn't cooperate either. The winds and current that made it easy enough to get to Bojador made it particularly difficult to get back, especially in a small, single-masted ship. No wonder no one volunteered to be the first beyond. The danger of being trapped seemed too real.

But Henry was getting tired of listening to excuses. Early in 1433 he decided to send Gil Eanes, one of his most trusted squires, with a clear mandate to sail beyond Bojador. Eanes left and sailed a southerly course, but once within sight of the cape his crew refused to go on, claiming they could see the water boiling. It left Eanes no choice but to return. Besides, it wasn't as if he himself was that keen to go on anyway. Seen through the fog in the distance, the sandstone cliffs beyond Bojador struck him as a formidable barrier. It didn't take a great deal of imagination to picture all kinds of unpleasant things there.

Upon his return to Lagos Eanes presumably got an earful for deferring to the fears of his crew. Azurara described what followed as if he were there:

> Now this was in the year of Jesus Christ 1433, and in the next year the Infant made ready the same vessel and, calling Gil Eanes apart, charged him earnestly to strain every nerve to pass that Cape. "You cannot find," said the Infant, "a peril so great that the hope of reward will not be greater. Go forth and make your voyage straightforward, inasmuch as with the grace of God you cannot but gain from this voyage honor and profit."

Henry was "a man of great authority," Azurara added, "so that his admonitions, mild though they were, had much effect on the serious-minded."

And so indeed they did. Eanes set out again and headed south. His predecessors usually steered for the coast once they reached the Canary Islands, but Eanes decided to take a different route. He stayed out at sea and kept to that course for a few days. Once he felt that he had sailed far enough, he headed east again, toward the African coast. He knew the ship had sailed beyond

Northwest Africa's desolate coast stretches on for hundreds of miles, proving a difficult challenge to the first explorers.

Cape Bojador, and thus far no calamity had befallen them. His confidence grew.

The following day the coast was sighted, and Eanes drew near. Though the land was barren, it was by no means forbidding, so he went

ashore with a few of his men. There were no signs of life other than a few plants. Eanes collected some, realizing that Henry would want some proof of his achievement. He called them the roses of Saint Mary. By the time he got back to Portugal there probably were no more than a few dried-out leaves left, but Henry reportedly treasured them as a gift from heaven.

We don't have any information on Eanes's return trip, though he presumably sailed back along the coast to explore it

Cape Bojador was rounded in 1434. Its size seems to suggest it stuck out more in myth than in reality.

and figure out how far he had gone beyond Bojador. Along the way he noticed that the horrors described with such macabre relish by earlier chroniclers were no more than figments of the medieval imagination. There were no monsters; in fact, there was hardly any life to speak of. Although the winds and currents ran the wrong way, they certainly didn't trap anyone. And the boiling water near the cape turned out to be no more than waves breaking over a rocky outcrop.

In terms of distance, Eanes's voyage wasn't a long one, no more than fifty to sixty miles beyond Cape Bojador. And yet it probably ranks as one of the most important voyages of the Age of Exploration. Gil Eanes indeed passed far more than a physical barrier. He had crossed the border between myth and reality. With that step taken, Henry's systematic program of exploration could finally begin in earnest.

We don't know whether Azurara was present when Eanes returned, though he seems to imply it:

> After he had finished giving an account of his voyage, the Infant caused another ship to be made ready, in which he sent Affonso Gonçalves Baldaia, his cupbearer, as well as Gil Eanes and his ship, ordering him to return there with his companions.
>
> And so, in fact, they did, passing fifty leagues beyond the Cape where they found the land without dwellings, but showing footmarks of men and camels.

Though mentioned offhandedly, this was revolutionary news. It shattered the long-held belief that there was no life beyond Bojador. There clearly were people here, and as Henry correctly surmised, a lot could be learned from them.

> "As you have found traces of men and camels," said the Infant to Baldaia, "it is clear that the inhabited region cannot be far off. Therefore I intend to send you there again, so that you can do me service and increase your honor, and to this end I order you to go as far as you can and try to gain an interpreter from among those people. It will not be a small gain if we can get someone to give us some tidings of the land."

Baldaia did as told, sailing to the mouth of a wide river some seventy miles beyond the previous landfall. Assuming that it led straight to the African interior and its fabled gold fields, he called it the Rio de Ouro, though there was no gold anywhere in sight—just a massive herd of seals basking along its banks. There were no signs of human habitation either, but Baldaia had brought along some horses to explore further inland. He ordered two young men to search the area and report back to him by evening.

Diogo Lopes and Heitor Homen followed the river and soon sighted footprints. Before long they caught up with a group of natives, but rather than cautiously approaching them and indicating peaceful intentions, the two youths promptly attacked. Terrified, the natives scattered in all directions and vanished. Unable to find them, Lopes and Homen were forced to return to the ship alone.

The Portuguese returned to the site the following day but, aside from a few meager belongings, there was no trace of the natives. Baldaia was convinced they had missed their chance. The sudden appearance of white-faced men on horses had undoubtedly caused such a scare that none of the natives were likely to return for some time. Not wanting to sail back empty-handed, Baldaia turned his men loose on the seals along the banks of the estuary. "They made among those wolves a very great slaughter," Azurara later reported. Though not exactly what Henry had asked for, their skins were something that could be sold back home and help defray the cost of the voyages.

"We did not find anything noteworthy to report," Azurara wrote of the next five years, implying that Henry had other things on his mind. He did indeed.

In 1433, his father died at the age of seventy-seven. The crown was passed to Edward, Henry oldest brother, who didn't prove as able a ruler as his father. While sincere and conscientious, Edward was more of a scholar and philosopher than the hard-headed ruler Portugal needed. His reign, as a result, was short and unhappy.

With his brother on the throne, Henry abandoned his exploratory efforts in favor of another plan to attack North Africa. This time the target was the city of Tangier, one of the principal Moorish bases in the area. The plan had been rejected by John I as being far too costly and risky, but with Edward in power Henry saw his chance. He schemed and cajoled and even got the pope to issue a bull of absolution for any-one who died in the struggle against the infidel. Edward harbored doubts about the venture, but eventually Henry convinced him. Reminded of the prestige which the sacking of Ceuta had yielded the Portuguese crown, the new king allowed the enterprise to go forward.

Unfortunately, the Tangier campaign turned into a disaster. If Henry had applied a bit of patience the outcome might have been different, but he proceeded with a hasty, ill-planned campaign, acting as if the fall of Tangier was a foregone conclusion. It proved a huge mistake. At one point, his army was surrounded by a vastly superior Moorish force. To avoid total annihilation, the Portuguese had to agree to a truce. The Moors demanded the surrender of Ceuta in return for safe-con-duct and took Prince Ferdinand hostage. Henry never saw his youngest brother again. The Portuguese refused to surrender their North African base, and the prince died in a Moorish dungeon five years later.

The army's return to Portugal differed sharply from the triumphant affair that followed the conquest of Ceuta more than twenty years ear-lier. There were no welcoming throngs of people or jubilant thanks-giving masses. Instead there was sadness over those who had lost their lives and a deep concern over the fate of young Prince Ferdinand. To Henry in particular it proved a humiliating experience. Saddened and disillusioned, he returned to the Algarve, becoming somewhat of a recluse. His oldest brother took the news even harder. In 1438, just a year after the Tangier debacle, King Edward died, creating "great dis-cords in the kingdom," as Azurara succinctly put it.

With Edward's son Afonso no more than six at the time, Pedro became regent, albeit after a protracted struggle for power. Henry tried to stay out of the political intrigue, but his brother needed him in Lisbon. As a result, his ships remained in port. This simply was not the time to carry on with the exploration of the African coast.

But the time was not all wasted. While Henry was preoccupied with political matters, his mariners considered ways to improve their ships. Eanes and Baldaia, who had sailed beyond Bojador, had found that their square-sailed ships were difficult to sail back against adverse winds and currents. With plenty of time on their hands, they began to experiment. The sails on Arab ships and Venetian galleys were known to point higher into the wind, so one of Henry's ships was equipped with a lateen sail to see how it would perform. Then a second mast with another lateen sail was added, and the hull was adjusted to accommodate the new sail plan. Its draft was kept shallow, to allow the ship to approach the coast without fear of grounding. Eanes and Baldaia knew that was essential to the process of exploration.

The caravel was a ship uniquely suited for exploration.

This interaction among Henry's mariners and shipwrights gradually led to a new type of ship. Relatively small and light, the caravel was a swift vessel. The lateen rig enabled it to make some headway into the wind, essential along the African coast. The shallow draft allowed it to nudge in and out of coves and bays and to explore rivers.

Nothing is known about the people involved in the design, but one can imagine Henry's mariners taking her out to check how she performed in various conditions and returning with suggestions to adjust this or that. We don't know whether Henry was involved, although such work probably wouldn't have been done without at least his tacit approval. Despite the disaster at Tangier and the discord that followed the death of Edward, he hadn't given up on his plans. All Henry needed was some stability, a chance to head back to Lagos and continue what really interested him more than anything else.

By the early 1440s, the political situation in Portugal had stabilized. Gratefully, Henry returned to Lagos, intent to pick up the pace of exploration. His brother too was interested in the sea route to Africa, which boded well for Henry's plans. Some of his long-standing curiosity was about to be satisfied.

"I think I can now take some sort of pleasure in the narrating of this history," Azurara declared when picking up the story.

Now it was so that in this year 1441, when the affairs of this realm were somewhat more settled though not fully quieted, that the Infant armed a little ship, of which he made captain one Antão Gonçalves, his chamberlain, and a very young man; and the end of that voyage was none other, according to my Lord's commandment, but to ship a cargo of the skins and oil of those seawolves. But it cannot be doubted that the Infant gave him the same charge that he gave to others, but as the age of this captain was weaker and his authority but slight, so the Prince's orders were less stringent, and in consequence his hopes of results less confident.

When he had accomplished his voyage, Antão Gonçalves called all the others that were in the ship, being twenty one in all, and spoke to them. "We have already got our cargo, and we may well turn back if we wish not to toil beyond what was commanded of us. But I would like to know from all of you whether we should attempt something further, for I think it would be shameful if we went back into the Infant's presence just as we are, having done such small service. How fair a thing it would be if we, who have come to this land for a cargo of such petty merchandise, were to meet with the good luck to bring the first captives before the face of our Prince."

As soon as it was night Gonçalves chose nine men who seemed most fitted for the undertaking. Journeying through the inner land for the space of three leagues, they found the footmarks of men and youths, the number of whom they estimated to be from forty to fifty, but they led the opposite way from where our men where going. The heat was very intense, and so by reason of this and the toil they had undergone in traveling on foot, Antão Gonçalves said "My friends, there is nothing to do here; our toil is great, while the profit from following up this path seems small for these men are traveling to the place whence we have come."

Yet while returning towards the sea, when they had gone a short part of the way, they saw a man following a camel. Though he was only one, and saw that the others were many, he began to defend himself as best he could, showing a bolder front than his strength warranted. But a man wounded him with a javelin, and this put the Moor in such fear that he threw down his arms like a beaten thing.

On the way back to the ship, they encountered an older woman whom they also captured. Both prisoners were taken to the ship, and the crew began to make preparations to head back for Portugal. But just as they were ready to haul anchor, they spied a sail on the horizon. It turned out to be the young knight Nuno Tristão, in command of the first caravel to be sent south.

Tristão had obviously received orders to get more than seal skins. He was pleased to hear that his colleague had succeeded in capturing some natives, but upon hearing that there were others in the vicinity, he felt compelled to get more. Wouldn't it be better, he suggested, if we carried off enough people so that, aside from gaining their knowledge, "profit will accrue by their service or ransom."

Tristão headed inland with some of his sailors, found a group of people, and attacked them. Several natives were killed in the skirmish, the rest—ten in all—were taken captive. The two ships then sailed on as far as Cape Blanco, where Tristão's men went ashore to capture even more people. But they found none, and decided to head back to Portugal.

> I cannot behold the arrival of these ships, with the novelty of the gain of those slaves before the face of our Prince, without finding some delight in the same. For just insofar as things are more desired, and more numerous and heavy labors are undergone for them, so much greater the delight they bring when a man obtains them. Now, seeing the beginnings of some recompense, may we not think you felt joy, not so much for the number of the captives taken, as for the hopes you conceived of the others you could take?
>
> But your joy was solely from that one holy purpose to seek salvation of the lost souls of the heathen. And in the light of this it appeared to you, when you saw those captives, that the expense and trouble was nothing. Such was your pleasure in beholding them. And yet the greater benefit was theirs, for though their bodies were now brought into some subjection, that was a small matter in comparison to their souls, which now possess true freedom for evermore.

Azurara's description, while brief, provides a great deal of insight. In retrospect, Tristão's commitment to capture more people so that "profit will accrue by their service" marked the onset of a black chapter in African history: the direct European involvement in the continent's slave trade. Slavery was nothing new, of course, and Azurara expressed delight at the prospect of profits—a return on investment, so to speak—but he tempered it with a moral perspective. Henry, he explained, wasn't interested in the profits as much as in the salvation of the heathen. Whether this was true remains a matter of debate, because the prince couldn't afford the business of exploration without financial returns. But there is little doubt that religion played a vital role. In fact, it provided not only the motivation but also a convenient justification once Europe's incursions began to tear away people from their homes.

After the first captives were brought to Portugal, the pace of exploration picked up. Both Antão Gonçalves and Nuno Tristão led a number of expeditions that progressed far beyond Bojador. In 1443 they reached the islands of Arguin and Tider, just north of the twentieth parallel. Though the coast remained uninviting, there were more people here: poor fishermen mostly, who subsisted on whatever the sea yielded. A few were captured, and reports of many more naturally made their way back to Portugal.

Later the same year, the regent granted his brother the exclusive right to sail beyond Bojador. According to a contemporary chronicler, it was well deserved. Henry had begun "to send out ships to acquaint themselves with the part of the world that lay beyond Cape Bojador because until then no one in all Christiandom had gone there and no one knew if it was peopled or not. Neither were there any true navigation charts nor maps of the world further south than Cape Bojador showing these things, other than those drawn to the mapmaker's imagination. And because it was an unknown part and men feared to go there, he sent ships to that part of the earth more than fourteen times and on two occasions brought back thirty-eight Moorish prisoners. He ordered a navigational chart to be drawn up and told us that he wished to send his ships further south in order to learn about the aforementioned land."

The grant enabled Henry to license the business of exploration, something the prince, as a shrewd businessmen, no doubt found appealing. He knew there would be takers. With small quantities of gold dust and other trading goods beginning to make their way back to

Portugal and, with the blessing of the Church, a clear potential to acquire slaves, some merchants had begun to express an interest in investing. In 1444, the first privately sponsored expedition consisting of no less than six ships took off from Lagos. Its crews obviously were not as interested in exploration as they were in making a quick profit, and that they proceeded to do. After raiding several villages on Arguin Island, they returned with two hundred captives.

The day after they arrived in Lagos, an impromptu slave market was held in a meadow outside the city. It was the first of many that would follow. From his description, it is clear that Azurara was present:

> Let my tears not wrong my conscience, for I wept in pity for their sufferings. For what heart could be so hard as to not be pierced with feelings to see that company. Some kept their heads low and their faces bathed in tears; others stood groaning very dolorously, looking up at the height of heaven; others struck their faces with the palms of their hands, throwing themselves at full length upon the ground; yet others made their lamentations after the custom of their country.
>
> Then, to increase their sufferings even more, there now arrived those who were in charge of dividing the captives and who began to separate one from another. Then it was needful to part fathers from sons, husbands from wives, brothers from brothers.
>
> Who could finish that partition without very great toil? For as soon as they had placed them in one part the sons, seeing their fathers in another, rushed over to them; the mothers clasped their children in their arms and threw themselves on the ground with them.
>
> The Infant was there, mounted on a powerful steed. He received his share as a man who sought to gain little from his share, for the forty-six souls that fell to him he offered to the Church. He reflected with great pleasure of those souls that before were lost.

In 1444 Dinis Dias reached Cape Verde, Africa's westernmost point.

Like the Africans that had preceded them here, these people were eventually integrated into Portuguese society. Azurara observed they were treated well, with some being adopted as daughters or even made heirs of their masters' wealth. "I never saw chains on any of these slaves," he wrote, "and more than once I have been invited by their owners to witness their baptism or marriage." But they were the lucky ones, treated humanely perhaps because they were among the first or because Henry set an example. In his presence no one dared to mistreat the captives.

Aside from licensing private voyages, the prince continued to send out his own men, with specific instructions to progress beyond the point reached by whoever preceded them. In 1444, Nuno Tristão reached the Senegal River and entered the "land of the Blacks," as it was called. It was more than a geographical border. North of it the landscape was bleak, even desolate, with people mostly of Moorish descent. South of it began the tropical forest, inhabited by blacks. Later that year, Dinis Dias sailed past Cape Verde, Africa's western-most point, and discovered the island of Gourée near present-day Dakar. The following year Álvaro Fernandes sailed as far as the Cape of Masts, near the Gambia River.

Private voyagers were request-ed to explore and chart unknown territory as well, but most found it far more profitable to raid a known coast than to scurry in and out of muddy estuaries in pursuit of geographical knowledge. In 1445, no fewer than four expedi-tions, a total of twenty-six ships, left Portugal. Most never made it to unknown territory, halting instead near Arguin Island to raid local vil-lages. Despite his earlier compassion for the captives, Azurara glorified these exploits, speaking of joyful victories and providing a regular head count of the number of infidels captured or killed, with the first pre-ferred to the latter, "for if they had been killed, the profit would not have been so great."

In the mid-1440s the Portuguese reached the Casamansa in southern Senegal. Exploring its many rivers proved a dangerous task.

Beyond Arguin, in tropical Africa and its forests, the going became tougher. News of the white men's raiding had spread ahead of their arrival, and this inevitably led to a number of confrontations. In 1446, for instance, Nuno Tristão sailed as far as the Gambia River and boarded one of the ship's boats to explore upriver. After penetrating deep into the mysterious forest, he and his companions made ready to return to their caravel but were ambushed by natives and hit by a shower of poisonous arrows. Four men died before they reached the ship; the rest succumbed later. Eighteen men, including Tristão, were buried at sea. No more than five sailors were left to man the ship, but they made it back to Portugal with news of the tragedy.

A hundred years after their arrival, the Portuguese established a small trading post in Cacheu in today's Guinea Bissau. A small fortress reminds us of their early presence here.

Henry was deeply affected by Tristão's death. Azurara, too, provided a moving tribute, "giving to his divine soul the primary seat of celestial glory as the first who for God's sake were to meet their end in that land." It was more than a eulogy for a single man. It was a tribute to the men from Henry's household, "noble knights," as he called them, who went to Africa with their minds set on glory. And it was a eulogy for a passing age, for now these knights and their medieval quest for God and truth were beginning to be replaced by merchants, far more interested in trade and profit.

A year later the Danish knight Abelhart, who had come to Portugal to partake in the voyages to Africa, met a similar fate near Cape Verde. He and a number of his men were massacred while exchanging gifts on the beach. Only one man managed to escape the ambush. Others, too, lost their lives, after the natives figured out how to resist the incursions.

Despite these losses, Henry's scheme of exploration was, in most respects, working. By 1448 some fifty ships had set sail for Africa; they had rounded its westernmost point and progressed as far as Bissau, and they had begun to bring back trade goods. Slaves proved the most profitable. Azurara, always interested in head counts, tells us that 927 of them had been brought to Portugal, generating revenues as well as self-righteous satisfaction over the number of lost souls brought onto the true path. Other goods also made their way back, in exchange, according to one chronicler, for leather, rough cloth, and blankets from Alentejo. To facilitate this exchange, the Portuguese built a small fortress on Arguin Island. It was the first European settlement along the West African coast.

Azurara concluded his narrative that year, after recording almost every voyage up to that point. Before finishing, he indicated an intent to write a second part to the chronicle, but never got to it. As a result, we don't know much about what occurred during the following years, although Henry's efforts were undoubtedly affected by new and serious "discords in the kingdom," as Azurara diplomatically put it.

It was around this time that Pedro's regency experienced increasing opposition from Portugal's aristocracy. Realizing that the impressionable young crown prince would be far easier to manipulate than the regent, Pedro's opponents pushed for Afonso to take up the reins of power. Flattered by the attention, the crown prince agreed, and in 1448 the regent was relieved of his duties. The resulting controversy came to a sad conclusion one year later, when Pedro was killed in a battle against his opponents.

Pedro's death deeply affected Henry, for now none of his brothers were left. Edward had died ten years earlier, Ferdinand ended his days as a Moorish prisoner in 1443, and now Pedro, with whom he probably got along best, was gone as well.

Though Henry had chosen his brother's side, he managed to survive the upheaval. Known as a recluse, he wasn't perceived as a threat to political stability. Pedro's opponents knew the prince was far more interested in exploring the unknown than in ruling the country. Besides, it was thought wise to have at least one of King John's sons live out his days naturally.

Cape St. Vincent near Sagres in southern Portugal. It was here that Henry the Navigator established himself towards the end of his life.

By the early 1450s, Henry was spending most of his time in the Algarve, on his estate at Raposeira, or in the small palace he had begun to construct on the Cape of St. Vincent at Sagres.

He was there in the spring of 1454, for instance, when Venice's annual Flanders fleet was delayed nearby because of contrary winds. Upon hearing that the Venetian galleys were anchored near Sagres, Henry sent one of his secretaries to the ships with samples of African trading goods, presumably to entice some of the merchants who were aboard and thus attract foreign capital. Like a competent salesman, the secretary talked of "seas which had never been sailed" and newly discovered lands "where marvels abound." To round off his pitch, he mentioned that there was a lot of money to be made in Africa, with merchants regularly making five to ten times their investment.

Aboard was Alvise da Cadamosto, a young Venetian merchant, who was very intrigued by the presentation. Admitting that the various products sparked "a great desire to go thither," he made further inquiries and found out that foreigners were allowed to venture into African waters, provided they put up some of the capital. "Having learnt all this," he later wrote, "I definitely made up my mind to go, for I was young, well-fitted to sustain all hardships, desirous of seeing the world and things never seen before by our nation, and I hoped also to draw from its honor and profit."

Cadamosto, as a result, never made it to Flanders. Before long he was on his way to Africa instead, observing and taking notes along the way. A few years later, the young Venetian published his impressions in a book. Right from the first paragraph we know we are in for something quite different from Azurara.

> I, Alouisa Da Cadamosto, was the first of that noble city of Venesia that was moved to sail the ocean sea beyond the Strait of Zibeltera towards the south in the land of the blacks of lower Ethiopia. On this my journey I saw many things new and worthy of some notice. In order that those that come after me may be able to understand what my thoughts were in the midst of varied things in strange new places—for truly both our customs and lands, in comparison with those seen by me, might be called another world—I decided that it would be laudable to make some record of them.

It turned out to be a laudable effort indeed. Here was a young merchant, interested not only in business but in just about anything he heard and saw: the people, their homes, what they ate, how they lived. Azurara, in contrast, hardly mentioned Africa or the Africans, except toward the end of his chronicle, almost as an afterthought.

Of course, it is not entirely fair to compare the two narratives. Azurara was old when his wrote his chronicle, whereas Cadamosto was young, energetic, and eager to see the world. Naturally, they would look at the same things with different eyes. Azurara also was a court historian, commissioned to write official documents; Cadamosto a pri-

vate merchant who didn't have to worry about the reactions of his superiors. Finally, aside from visits to Ceuta and Alcázar Seguer, Azurara never set foot in Africa, which forced him to rely on the reports of others. Cadamosto, in contrast, spent a good bit of time in Africa during the course of two voyages.

The first of these left in 1455. As did most ships at that time, they stopped at the small fortress at Arguin, providing the young merchant a chance to explore the region and its trade. Always looking for good business opportunities, he noted that the local Arabs regularly came to the coast with slaves from the "land of the Blacks" and with gold dust, which they traded for cloth, carpets, and especially wheat, "for they are always short of food." Cadamosto also described the people, though it is not a flattering portrait: "They are a very poor people, liars, the biggest thieves in the world and exceedingly treacherous." The fact that they rubbed their hair with fish oil, something they considered "a great refinement," presumably didn't do much to improve that impression.

Further south the young Venetian grew more enthusiastic, perhaps because so much of what he saw was totally new and exciting. At the mouth of the Senegal River, he got to know Budomel, a local chieftain who ruled the southern bank of the river. They agreed to trade, and Budomel invited Cadamosto to his village. It was an invitation the young merchant could hardly refuse for, as he put it, "my journey inland was indeed more to see interesting sights and obtain information, than to receive my dues." The result is the first direct European look at West African life five hundred years ago.

"Four or five take their places in the field equipped with spades, and advance throwing the soil before them . . ." The tilling practices described by Cadamosto are still employed in West Africa.

This is what I was able to observe of this lord and his manners, and his house.

First, I saw clearly that, though these pass as lords, it must not be thought that they have castles or cities. The king of this realm had nothing save villages of grass huts, and Budomel was lord only of a part of his realm. Such men are not lords by virtue of treasure or money, but on account of ceremonies and the following of people they may truly be called lords. Indeed they receive beyond comparison more obedience than our lords.

After getting local politics out of the way, Cadamosto turned his eye to local resources, especially agricultural.

No wheat, rye, barley, or vines grow in this Kingdom, nor from thence onwards, in any regions of the land of the blacks. This is because the country is very hot and without rain for nine months of the year, that is from October to the end of June. It appears that they grow various kinds of millet, beans, and kidney beans, which are the largest and finest in the world.

Their method of working is as follows: four or five of them take their places in the field equipped with small spades, and advance throwing the soil before them, a practice contrary to that of our laborers who when tilling the soil draw it towards them. Here they throw it forward with their spades and do not penetrate more than four inches or so. This is their methods of agriculture, and since the ground is fertile and rich, it brings forth the things described before.

As befits a good businessman, Cadamosto also examined the region's livestock. He inquired about wildlife as well, realizing that people back home would want to hear about these things.

There are no domestic animals other than bulls, cows, and goats. No sheep are bred, nor could they live here on account of the great heat. The cows and bulls of this country (and also of all the land of the blacks) are very much smaller than ours (I believe this is as a result of the heat).

Wild beasts of prey are lions and lionesses, and leopards in great numbers. There are also wild elephants. These animals go in herds, as our swine do in the forests. Of their size I shall say nothing, for I believe everyone must know that the elephant is an animal with a very large body and short limbs. I understand that in these lands there are giraffes, and other animals of the most savage kinds.

There are large numbers of snakes, great and small. Some are

". . . enormous quantities of white ants, which by instinct make houses . . ."
Cadamosto was referring to termites.

poisonous, others not. Of the bigger some are two paces and more in length, but without wings or feet which serpents [are said to] possess. They are so large that snakes are found which swallow a goat whole, without tearing it to pieces. It is said that these great ones are found in swarms in some parts of the country, where there are also enormous quantities of white ants, which by instinct make houses for these snakes with sand which they carry in their mouths. Of these houses they make a hundred to a hundred and fifty in one spot, like fine towns.

The port of Bissau. Cadamosto sailed as far as this area on his second trip to Africa.

On the way back from Budomel's territory, Cadamosto encountered two other caravels, one of them commanded by another Italian, the Genoan Antonio Usodimare. The two captains decided to join forces and progressed beyond Cape Verde, looking for new trade opportunities. But it was rough going. South of the cape they watched one of their interpreters being hacked to pieces by the natives, indicating that the trading potential here was likely to remain limited. The Gambia River, where Nuno Tristão had been killed ten years earlier, proved hardly more welcoming. Whenever the ships entered the river, they were met by war canoes, each one filled with thirty fearless warriors. It wasn't very safe, but here too Cadamosto proved a keen observer, describing the canoes and the paddling techniques, admitting that the Gambians managed to propel their vessels "exceedingly swiftly."

Given the unfriendly reception, there was nothing to do but turn back and head for Portugal, but Cadamosto made up his mind to return and check out the area. A year later he did, accompanied once more by Usodimare and a third caravel commanded by one of Henry's captains.

This time the Portuguese received a less hostile reaction, and Cadamosto managed to visit a chief some sixty miles inland along the Gambia River. But the trading potential proved disappointing: cotton, thread, and baboons and other apes, Cadamosto reported, knowing he wasn't going to strike it rich with that. Even so, he never lost interest in the surroundings. Elephants, and especially the methods for hunting them, were elaborately described, the young merchant clearly fascinated by the operation. He even got to try the meat but described it as tasteless.

Cadamosto also focused a good bit of attention on the people themselves. To Azurara the Africans were either infidels or blacks, who attained a personality only if and when they were captured and converted. Cadamosto, in contrast, described people regardless of their beliefs. It wasn't always a flattering description, but it certainly proved far more interesting than Azurara's simple division between believers and unbelievers.

During his travels Cadamosto also observed how Africans reacted to European technology, telling us how they "marveled greatly at many of our possessions." Cannons, of course, frightened them, accounting for their designation as an invention of the devil. The bagpipe, on the other hand, they called a divine instrument, "made by God with his own hands, for it sounded so sweetly with so many different voices." The Africans were also greatly impressed by European ships and nautical methods, calling the sailors great wizards, almost the equal of the devil. And simple things caused wonderment: the light of a candle, for instance, was seen as "beautiful and miraculous." Cadamosto taught them how to make candles from beeswax, which made the locals exclaim that "we Christians had knowledge of everything."

In many ways, Cadamosto represented the type of explorer Henry had always wanted: a man who established friendly relations with the natives in order to promote legitimate trade. Unfortunately, among Henry's emissaries there were few such men. Some of his own knights perceived exploration as a crusade, with the number of "savages" brought onto the "true path" clearly more important than geographical knowledge. Commercial captains often ignored their orders alto-

The Bijagos islands in today's Guinea Bissau.

gether and took off on excursions of their own, capturing people or encouraging others to do so and creating such havoc that it would take years to rebuild some measure of trust. To Africans, as to most people, the first impression was a defining one. Most Europeans didn't leave a very good one.

After Cadamosto and Usodimare, Henry sent out Diogo Gomes, another Portuguese and probably a member of his household. Gomes's report has much in common with Cadamosto's. It appears

The Bijagos islands in today's Guinea Bissau are West Africa's largest archipelago. Discovered by Cadamosto around 1457, they remain one of the region's most isolated areas.

that he left in 1457 and also went as far as the Gambia, claiming to have reached the market town of Cantor, where he met traders from Mali and Timbuktu. Gomes also established friendly relations with some of the local chieftains and, when some of them expressed an interest in Christianity, promised to send priests. A year later Henry fulfilled that promise, and dispatched the first priest to the Gambia.

In 1459 Gomes set sail again, this time teaming up with two other caravels off Cape Verde. On the return trip the small fleet sailed far to the west of Africa to explore a group of islands Cadamosto claimed to have sighted a few years earlier. Like Madeira and the Azores before, these proved uninhabited and thus good candidates for colonization. The king agreed, appointing the Genoese captain Antonio da Noli, who reached Lisbon with the news, the first governor of the Cape Verde islands.

The following year another voyage was sent south. According to one of the crew members, the two caravels reached the Bijagós Islands in today's Guinea-Bissau. Though he didn't accompany the trip, Cadamosto included an account of it in his narrative:

They went to these islands, upon one of which they landed and spoke with the blacks, but were unable to understand them. They also visited their dwellings some distance inland, miserable huts of straw. In some of those they found wooden idols, from which they concluded that these blacks were idolators. Not being able to obtain anything nor to understand these people, they left them and continued their voyage along the coast until they reached the mouth of a great river, some fifty miles along the coast beyond the mouth of the Rio Grande.

Departing thence and sailing on, they came to a cape which

they called Cape Verga. All the coast is mountainous, though not
of great height. The mountains are covered with very beautiful,
large, and tall trees, and appear very green from a great distance—
a very pleasant sight to the eye.

They passed this Cape Verga, and sailing along the coast for
about eighty miles, discovered another cape, which in the opinion
of all the sailors was the loftiest cape they had ever seen. In the
middle of this cape there is a high point, in the shape of a dia-
mond. The whole is covered with very tall, green trees. They
named it Cape Sagres, after a fort which was built by the Infant
Henry in Portugal.

But by that time, their great sponsor was no more. At Sagres in
southwestern Portugal, Henry had put his affairs in order. Aware that
death was approaching, he transferred his estates and revenues to his
nephew and appointed heir and arranged for masses to be said for his
soul. His last will was signed October 28, 1460. Two weeks later, on
November 13, he died peacefully.

We have a report of it from Diogo Lopes, who was nearby:

On the night he died, his body was taken to St. Mary's church
in Lagos, where he was buried with full honors. King Afonso was
in Evora at the time. He and all his people were deeply saddened
by the death of such a great lord who had been so wealthy, had
owned everything coming from Guinea, spent such fortunes on
war, and had conducted naval warfare against the Moors for the
Christian faith.

At the end of the year, the King called me because, on his
orders, I had stayed in Lagos to be close to the Prince's body and
to check upon the priests who were told to provide constant vig-
ils and perform divine rites. The King ordered me to see whether
the Prince's corpse had reached a state of decomposition because
it was his wish to transfer the bones to a beautiful monastery called
St. Mary of Victory which had been built by his father, John I,
together with the monks of the preaching order.

Going to the body, I discovered it to be dry and intact except
for the tip of the nose. And I found it wrapped around in coarse
horse-hair sacking. Until his death, Prince Henry was a virgin and
during his life, such was the number of his good deeds that it
would be impossible to count them all.

Then the king sent his brother and bishop and counts to

accompany the body to the Batalha monastery where the king was waiting to receive the body of the deceased.

And Prince Henry was entombed in a large and very beautiful chapel that his father, King John, had built, and where the king himself, Queen Philippa, his wife and Prince Henry's mother, and five of his brothers all lay.

May their memory be eternally praised. And may they rest in pace. Amen.

Henry's death brought Portugal's exploratory activities to a halt. Despite the accolades, King Afonso was far more interested in fighting the Moors than in continuing his uncle's work. He knew he didn't need to sail to West Africa to pick a fight. That could be had much closer to home, across the Strait of Gibraltar.

As a result, only one exploratory voyage left Portugal during the early 1460s. Headed by Pêro de Sintra, it sailed as far as today's Sierra Leone. Here the coast began a clear curve towards the east, but no one followed up. As before, exploration required more than a set of favorable circumstances. It needed someone with vision to guide it onward. With Henry's death went the one person who, at that time, had the interest and capability to do so.

CHAPTER 2

Beyond the Cape of Storms

I am that mighty Cape hidden in mystery
The Cape of Storms you call it,
where Africa comes to an end.
I was unknown to all those of old.
Your daring offends it deeply.

> Luís de Camões
> *The Lusiads*, Canto V

Stretched along the northwest African coast are places like Ceuta, Alcázar Seguer, Tangier, and Arzila—all reminders of Portugal's erstwhile obsession with Morocco. There, tantalizingly close, were the despised infidels, and from the fall of Ceuta in 1415 many Portuguese nobles saw it as their duty to conquer as much of their land as possible.

Despite the disastrous outcome of the campaign to take Tangier in 1437, Henry remained one of the great proponents of military expansion in Morocco. But there wasn't a great deal he could do about it. His brother Pedro, who ruled the country as regent from 1441 to 1448, was all too aware of the costs of these expeditions, feeling they yielded few tangible benefits. Even Ceuta continued to be a massive drain on the treasury, because every so often the Moors mounted an expedition to retake the city, forcing supplies and reinforcements to be sent there.

As a result, little came of Henry's Moroccan plans during his brother's reign. But when his nephew took up the reins of power in 1448, the picture changed. In King Afonso V, Henry found someone who wholeheartedly shared his crusading spirit. When the young king expressed an interest in attacking the Moors in retaliation for the fall of Constantinople in 1453, his uncle offered eager advice. Henry may even have suggested another attempt on Tangier, but the court decided on the lesser fortress of Alcázar Seguer instead.

And so in 1458 another Portuguese fleet set sail for Morocco. Although sixty-four at the time, Henry was among the first to disembark. Much better prepared than the expedition to Tangier twenty years earlier, the invasion force quickly overpowered the defenders. Henry and the king jointly accepted their surrender and returned to

Portugal, after an absence of no more than a week. To Henry, in particular, the campaign must have brought much satisfaction. It helped erase bitter memories of the defeat at Tangier and brought him full circle—as a young knight he had fought bravely at Ceuta; more than forty years later he did so again at Alcázar Seguer.

Now Portugal had two bases in Morocco. It wasn't a sizable gain in territory, but, as before, size wasn't the issue.

Henry's death in 1460 didn't affect Afonso's interest in Morocco. The victory at Alcázar Seguer had given him a taste of glory, and he craved more. Afonso liked to see himself as a noble defender of the true faith, a king who personally led the fight against the hated Moors, and there was no place that could better be done than in Morocco, just across the Strait of Gibraltar. Aside from his courtiers, few people in Portugal shared that commitment, but the king wasn't one to defer to the opinion of his lowly subjects. Under his rule, Morocco became not only a personal obsession but a major foreign policy objective.

Accordingly, Portugal headed into a string of Moroccan adventures, many of them ill-planned. In 1463, the king was informed that there was a sewer under the walls of Tangier through which the city could be entered. It gave Afonso an excellent excuse to organize a military campaign. No effort was made to verify the story or to even keep the objective secret. Not surprisingly, things didn't go as planned. Spurred on by the king, the fleet left late in the year and was hit by a ferocious storm.

A few ruins remain of the fortress of Alcázar Seguer, site of Portugal's second conquest in Morocco.

When they finally arrived off Ceuta, many of those aboard were desperately ill and weakened. Though they had a brief respite in which to recover, it was not a good way to start the battle for Tangier.

Over the next several months a number of unsuccessful attempts were made to scale the city's walls. Frustrated, Afonso decided to attack the smaller city of Arzila, but that too proved impossible. A raid against some inland hill tribes almost turned into a disaster, with the king barely escaping with his life. The attempt on Tangier was called off.

Though Afonso had little to show for his efforts when the invasion force returned to Portugal, the king's resolve never wavered. When civil war broke out in Morocco in the late 1460s, he quickly seized the opportunity. He sent out observers who returned to tell him that Arzila was barely defended, since its forces were busy attacking the city of Fez. Afonso acted immediately. He organized an invasion force and headed for Morocco once more.

This time Arzila was an easy target. Though its remaining defenders put up a valiant fight, they were no match for the invasion force and were slaughtered to the last man. The city itself was sacked, its inhabitants killed or rounded up to be sold as slaves, and its buildings set aflame. After the battle, the king knighted his son John, who had distinguished himself in the fighting. It was reminiscent of the scene at Ceuta more than half a century earlier, when King John I knighted his sons— among them Henry—for valor on the battlefield. The similarity didn't end there. Prince John would play as much of a role in the story of the discoveries as his great-uncle did.

Arzila was conquered in 1471. It brought to three the number of Portuguese enclaves in North Africa.

Arzila brought to three the number of Portuguese enclaves in Morocco; a fourth quickly followed. Upon hearing of the city's fall and the slaughter among its inhabitants, the people of Tangier decided to surrender. A Portuguese force was sent to occupy it, handing Afonso the jewel in the North African crown. Bolstered by this unexpected series of victories, the king called himself "King of Portugal and the Algarves, both on this side and beyond the Sea." His subjects shortened it to Afonso the African, the name by which he became known to posterity.

Though Afonso's African perspective was largely confined to Morocco, his policies had a major effect on the rest of Africa as well. Fighting the Moors of North Africa was an expensive proposition. Ships had to be built or chartered, knights and soldiers had to be paid, and troops had to be supplied. These demands forced the king to dip deep into the treasury, with few if any chances of returns.

It was probably for this reason that Afonso began to take more of an interest in the trade with Africa, or Guiné, as it was called. Since the death of Henry there had been no further voyages of exploration, but trade with the region continued, with merchants occasionally sending ships to search for gold and slaves. According to historian João de Barros, writing in the mid-sixteenth century, they did a brisk business:

> At this time the trade of Guiné was already very current between our men and the inhabitants of those parts, and they carried on their business in peace and friendliness, without those warlike incursions, assaults, and robberies which happened at the beginnings—as could not have been otherwise with people so wild and barbarous, both in law and customs and in the use of the things of this our Europe.
>
> These people were always intractable. However, after they learned something of the truth through the benefits they received, both spiritual and intellectual, and articles for their use, they became so well disposed that when ships, sailing from this Kingdom, arrived at their ports, many people came from the interior to seek their goods, which they received in exchange for human beings, who were brought here more for salvation than for slavery.

Barros wrote this description for his *Decadas da Ásia*—a history of Portugal's overseas exploits that took no fewer than seventeen years, from 1550 to 1567, to complete. Much of it dealt with events that took place many years earlier, but as factor of the Casa da Índia in Lisbon, Barros had access to a variety of sources and documents, many of which have since been lost or destroyed. Besides, it is not that there is much of a choice. Barros often is the only source of information on Portugal's activities in Africa in the late fifteenth century.

Though written with the usual Western bias, Barros not only covered the Portuguese but also the peoples they encountered elsewhere. He didn't necessarily hold them in high esteem, but when Africans in turn expressed a poor opinion about their European visitors, he included that as well, providing a measure of even-handedness absent from earlier accounts. Even so, in many ways Barros hadn't progressed much beyond the attitudes of his predecessors. When people were traded, he still assumed that their salvation justified their enslavement. The fact that Portuguese merchants were making money selling them seemed merely incidental.

It wouldn't take long for the king to smell an opportunity here.

Desperate for income to finance his Moroccan exploits, Afonso decided to lease African exploration rights for cash. It is only through Barros that we know of this innovative deal.

> As the King was very occupied with the affairs of the Kingdom and was not satisfied to cultivate this trade himself nor let it run as it was, he leased it on request in 1469 to Fernão Gomes, a respected citizen of Lisbon, for five years at two hundred thousand reis a year, on condition that in each of these five years he should engage to discover one hundred leagues of coast farther on, so that at the end of the lease five hundred leagues should be discovered, beginning from Sierra Leone, where the last discoverers turned back.

For the court, this was a pure windfall: 200,000 reis for which the king had to do nothing but collect the fees. Aside from paying the license fee, Gomes also committed to progressing one hundred leagues (about 350 miles) into unknown territory each year. In return, he received the exclusive right to trade with any newfound regions, though some goods remained reserved to the Crown.

As Barros made clear, the lease proved an excellent way to restart the stalled exploration process:

Gomes's men sailed past Cape Palmas, where the African coast turns east again.

> Fernão Gomes was so diligent and fortunate that in January 1471 his agents João de Santarem and Pero de Escobar, both knights of the King's household, discovered the traffic of gold at the place we now call the Mina.
>
> But Fernão Gomes not only established this traffic of gold; his discoverers, under the terms of the contract, reached the Cabo de Santa Catharina, two and a half degrees South of the Equator.
>
> At this time (1474) one Fernão do Pó discovered the Ilha Formosa, which now bears the name of its discoverer. And the last discoverer in the life of King Dom Afonso was one Sequeira,

knight of his household, who discovered the cape which we call Cabo de Catharina, a name given to it because it was discovered on the day of this Saint.

The Ilha de São Thomé, Ano Bom, and Principe, were also discovered by order of the King Dom Afonso, and other trading places and islands, which we do not treat in detail because we do not know when or by which captains they were discovered; however, it is generally known that many more events happened and discoveries were made in the time of this King.

Gomes's men, in other words, did far better than the required five hundred leagues. In the five years between 1469 and 1474 they covered the two thousand miles between Sierra Leone and the easternmost point of the Gulf of Guinea, and then continued south as far as Cape St. Catherine, more than one hundred miles below the equator.

Unfortunately, we know very little about these voyages, other than the few names Barros mentions. Gomes, it appears, was interested mostly in fulfilling his part of the contract—covering at least one hundred leagues per year—and in making money from trade. He first sent out one Soeiro da Costa, who had sailed to Sierra Leone with Pêro de Sintra around 1460. Costa passed Cape Palmas, where the West African coast makes an intriguing turn to the east, and sailed beyond today's Abidjan. Along the way he examined the trading opportunities, finding malaguetta pepper, woven baskets, and, of course, slaves, which were traded for metals, cloth, and a variety of trinkets. There wasn't anything spectacular here, but in just one voyage, Gomes's mariners had met the requirements for several years' worth of exploring.

A year or so later, Gomes sent out João de Santarem and Pêro de Escobar who sailed beyond Cape Three Points in today's Ghana. On this trip, as Barros pointed out, the Portuguese finally struck gold. With rich alluvial deposits in the area and mines further north, there was a thriving gold trade along the coast, and Santarem quickly found out it could be had for almost nothing. Rather than continuing further along the coast, he returned to Lisbon with news of the discovery.

There is no question Gomes dispatched subsequent voyages to the area because he made a fortune off the trade, but he didn't neglect his lease requirements either. In 1472, one of his men discovered an island at the end of the Gulf of Guinea. He called it Ilha Formosa—beautiful island—but until recently it bore his name: Fernão do Pó. Here he must have noticed that the African coast resumed its southward trend, but we have no idea of how he reacted to that. There is no mention in any of the early chronicles of the coast beyond Cape Three Points. It appears that Pó and his colleagues were eager to put this marshy, unhealthy area behind them.

A year later Gomes sent out Rui de Sequeira, who crossed the equator in 1473 or 1474 and sailed past Cape Lopes as far south as Cape St. Catherine, in today's Gabon. On the trip home, Sequeira cut across the Gulf of Guinea, discovering the islands of Anno Bom, São Tomé, and Principe, several hundred miles off the African coast.

Having sailed well beyond the equator, Gomes's sailors added several thousand miles to the map of Africa, though it appeared that the coast once more stretched endlessly south. But Gomes did well in the process. Not only did he make a good deal of money, but in 1474— the final year of the lease—Afonso also knighted him. He received a new coat of arms—"a shield with crest and three heads of Negroes on a field of silver, each with golden rings in ears and nose, and a collar of gold around the neck, and Da Mina as a surname," as Barros described it, in honor of what would become one of Portugal's most important early discoveries.

By that time, the king had transferred the responsibility for Africa's trade and exploration to his son John, who took a serious interest in it. But political trouble interfered once more, diverting the young prince's attention. This time it was the resumption of war with Castile which brought the process of exploration to a temporary halt.

Peace between the two neighboring countries was concluded in September 1479, by which time Prince John had taken over many of the king's responsibilities. He was involved in negotiating the Treaty of Alcáçovas, for instance, making sure that, aside from settling any immediate differences with Castile, Portugal was given clear title to the Lordship of Guinea, as it was called, "and all its regions, lands, and markets, together with its gold mines, both those discovered or to be discovered, spoken or to be spoken of, and the islands of Madeira, Porto Santo, and Deserta, the Azores and Las Flores, the Cape Verde Islands, and all the islands which have been discovered, mentioned, or conquered from the Canaries southward." In this way John sought to preclude Castilian incursions in the trade, which had become a source of serious friction. Castile, in turn, received clear title to the Canary Islands.

With peace at hand and Portugal's claim to Africa firmly established, at least in the minds of the Iberian antagonists, John could turn

Fishermen at work on a Ghanan beach. Because of the active gold trade that took place along the coast, the area became known as the Gold Coast.

his attention to the business of exploration. In absence of supervision, the rich trade in gold with El Mina had begun to attract interlopers, and this was something he wanted to prevent. Merchant captains sailing for the Gold Coast were instructed to look for intruders and capture them so that they could be punished appropriately. It was the fate of one Eustace de la Fosse, a Frenchman who had sailed for El Mina in 1479. Intercepted on his way home, he and his crew were imprisoned and his goods and ship were confiscated.

When King Afonso died "of a fever" in August 1481, his son took up the reins of power, ascending the throne as John II. The new king quickly consolidated his power, rescinding many of his father's grants—a move that created a great deal of resentment among Portugal's nobility. He also directed attention to tropical Africa, deciding there was need for a permanent base near El Mina to facilitate and, especially, to protect the valuable gold trade. Accordingly he sent a fleet of twelve ships and what amounted to a pre-fabricated fortress to the region. Aboard were six hundred men—one hundred of them craftsmen, the others sailors and soldiers. They were led by Diogo de Azambuja, one of the king's most loyal and capable officers.

Upon arriving at the Gold Coast, Azambuja selected a sheltered bay some sixty miles west of today's Accra. The natives had grown used to Portuguese vessels by then, but establishing a base was a different matter. This called for negotiations with Kwamena Ansah, the local king, and both sides agreed to meet on the beach. The Portuguese wore court dress for the occasion, undoubtedly to impress Kwamena Ansah of the significance of the event. The Africans, deciding not to be outdone, showed up with a full complement of warriors and musicians, creating a racket "more deafening than pleasing to the ear," Barros later reported.

Through an interpreter, Diogo de Azambuja explained his mission, mentioning the king of Portugal's desire to have Kwamena Ansah baptized, to establish bonds of friendship with him and his people, and to continue the trade, all of which called for the building of "a strong house, in addition to quarters wherein to lodge the honorable people who accompanied him." Next he requested permission to build this "great house," adding that neighboring rulers "would consider it a great honor to have this fortress built in their lands."

There was no need to address Kwamena Ansah in such simple terms. He had already gathered why the Portuguese were there in such force and had his doubts about this "great house." As Barros put it, Azambuja and his men had made a better impression than their predecessors, whom the king described as "ill-dressed and ragged men only, who were content with whatever he gave them in exchange for their goods." But the African ruler felt that things ought to be kept the way they were, presenting his doubts in memorable terms:

> "Friends who met occasionally remained better friends than if they were neighbors, on account of the nature of the human heart—for it resembled the waves of the sea which, breaking upon a rock barring their path, were tossed up to the sky, so that a double mischief was done, the sea being turned to a fury and the rock, its neighbor, being damaged."

Despite Kwamena Ansah's misgivings, both sides eventually agreed that a "great house" be built. Azambuja lost no time in commencing the construction, as Barros reported:

> The work progressed so rapidly that in twenty days the outer wall of the castle was raised to a good height, and the tower to the first floor. On account of the special devotion of the King for the Saint, this fortress was called São Jorge, and it was later created a town, with all the respective liberties and privileges.
>
> When this work was finished, and trade begun in the country, Diogo de Azambuja sent back to the Kingdom the ships and the supernumeraries, with much gold that they had obtained, while he remained with the sixty men allotted to the fortress by the King's instructions. Others remained buried at the foot of the tree where the first Mass was said, which stood in the grounds of the church consecrated to São Jorge. There God is praised today, not only by our men who visit that town, but also by those Ethiopians who, having been baptized, are included among the faithful.

During the two years and seven months that Diogo de Azambuja was there, it pleased God that they did not suffer as much from disease as they had feared; and with so much prudence did he settle the prices and rules of the traffic that today the greater part of his regulations are still observed.

Though subsequently modified by the Dutch and the British, the fortress of El Mina still stands firmly along the Ghanian coast. Today it is remembered for its tragic past. Tens of thousands of slaves passed through here prior to being shipped across the Atlantic.

❧

While the fortress of São Jorge, the first European settlement in tropical Africa, was being built, John II also began to consider the further exploration of the African coast. Eight years had passed since Rui de Sequeira had crossed the equator, and the king felt it was time to send a new voyage south. He also gave it a clear purpose: the search for a passage to the Indies. What had until then been a vaguely defined, implied objective now became a matter of national policy.

The man chosen to head the mission was Diogo Cão, an experienced mariner who had sailed to El Mina on at least one occasion. Unfortunately, little is known about Cão and his voyages. Even historians writing a few years afterward were able to provide no more than a few remarks, presumably as a result of a growing policy of secrecy.

The king wanted to conceal information about Portugal's overseas activities from the outside world. He knew that others would be more than interested in a sea route to the Indies. The less they knew, the better.

From the few surviving sources, historians have determined that Cão probably left Lisbon in late August 1482. We know little about who or what was aboard, other than a set of stone pillars, designed to replace the wooden markers that had previously been set up on or near prominent landmarks. The ship first set sail for the newly completed fortress at El Mina, where Cão stopped to take on provisions. A few weeks later he passed Cape St. Catherine, and entered unknown territory.

Barros is one of the few sources to tell us what Cão did next:

> He reached a great river and on the southern bank of the estuary he set up the Pillar to indicate he was taking possession of all the coast north on behalf of the King. This Pillar was dedicated to St. George because the King had a singular devotion to that saint and for a long time the river was called the Pillar River.
>
> Later it was called the River Congo because it ran through a kingdom of that name discovered by Diogo Cão on that voyage.
>
> The natives also called it the river Zaire. It was all the more famous and great for its waters than for its name. In winter in those parts its flows so strongly into the sea that its fresh waters are found up to twenty leagues from the coast. Once Diogo Cão had set up the Pillar and seen the grandeur of this river at its estuary and its copious flow, he judged that such a mighty river valley would be very densely inhabited. He ventured upriver and saw that more people appeared on the bank than had done on previous occasions. They were all very black and had short curly hair. Diogo Cão's men understood some of the tongues of other peoples they had discovered but this time they were unable to understand anything and they had to resort to signs.

The coast of northern Angola was discovered on Diogo Cão's first voyage.

Ambriz, Angola. Once a thriving colonial town, it is now largely destroyed, a victim of Angola's devastating civil war.

They understood that these people had a very powerful King who was several days march inland. Diogo Cão saw how the people reacted and was aware of what they expected of him. He ordered some of our men to go with some of theirs bearing a gift to the King of that land, with the promise that they would return in so many days time. However the time went by and Diogo Cão received no message.

Cão, in other words, did exactly what was expected of him. He had been instructed to establish friendly relations with local rulers, so he sent his men to the king of Congo, known as the manicongo, who had his capital some fifty miles inland.

Founded in 1575, the Angolan capital of Luanda retains reminders of the Portuguese presence, including the fortress of São Miguel.

According to Barros and other chroniclers, he waited several months for his messengers to return but then grew impatient. So he decided to continue the voyage, sailing as far as Cape Santa Maria, nearly one hundred miles south of today's Benguela in Angola. There he erected another pillar—the only evidence of this part of the voyage. Returned to Lisbon in 1892, it bears the following inscription:

It was 6681 years after the creation of the world and 1482 years after the birth of Our Lord Jesus that the very exalted, very excellent, mighty prince King John the second of Portugal ordered this land to be discovered and these stone markers to be placed by Diogo Cão, squire of his house.

Either there or, possibly, somewhat further along the coast, Cão decided to turn back. Perhaps he was running short of supplies, or believed he was near the point where the African coast would again turn eastward. On the trip north he halted near the Zaire River to pick up the people who had been left behind, but they were nowhere to be found. Cão seized four Congolese hostages instead, explaining to their families that they would be returned safely "before fifteen moons." He then set a course for home.

Luanda is also home to several seventeenth-century churches.

Arriving in early 1484, a year and a half after setting out on what had become the longest voyage to that date, Cão received a cordial welcome. Though the coast at Cape Santa Maria runs more west than east, John apparently was convinced that the passage to the Indian Ocean was near. Accordingly, Cão was knighted and awarded a generous pension.

The king was eager to press on and dispatch a new voyage, but serious political problems in Portugal prevented him from doing so. Accordingly, it wasn't until the following year, when the situation had stabilized somewhat, that he called on Cão to head south again.

Cão left on this second voyage in the fall of 1485. Aboard were the four Congolese hostages seized on the first trip, all of them by now fluent in Portuguese, and Pêro de Escobar, who had sailed with Fernão Gomes more than ten years earlier. Also along was José Vizinho, one of the great astronomers of that time, to take measurements of the sun in the southern hemisphere. Taking a scientist on such a long and exhausting voyage was something new but essential, for it was impossible to determine a precise latitude without having accurate data on the declination of the sun.

Cão's first voyage took him as far as the coast of central Angola.

As before, Cão first sailed to El Mina to take on food and water. Then he set a course across the Gulf of Guinea towards the Zaire estuary. Barros wrote of their reception:

When Diogo Cão sailed back to the mouth of the Pillar River he was received with great pleasure by the local inhabitants on seeing their own men alive and so well treated. And obeying the order which King John had given him, he sent one of the four Negroes with some of the local natives whom he knew with a message for the King of Congo informing that he had returned with his subjects as promised. He requested that, as his King had ordered him to sail further down the coast in his service, the King of Congo should send him the Portuguese under one of his Captains and that he would hand over the other three of his subjects. He added that, when he returned safely, he would speak of other things that his King had commanded and that he would offer more presents from him.

Our men duly arrived escorted by a Captain sent by the King of Congo and Diogo Cão handed over the three natives along with gifts for the King. He took his leave and sailed south to discover other coasts.

Namibia's skeleton coast proved a major challenge. With food and water running low and few places ashore to provision, it became clear Cão's second voyage could not continue.

On this part of the voyage Cão passed his earlier marker at Cape Santa Maria, and went ashore 125 miles further south at Cape Negro to set up another one. Beyond, the coast took on an encouraging southeasterly slant but grew more desolate. The lush tropical forests seen along the northern Angolan coast were increasingly replaced by barren lands, more reminiscent of the desert regions of northwest Africa. Meanwhile, adverse currents and persistent southeast winds began to hinder the ship's progress. With every passing day, the going became tougher.

Nonetheless, Cão moved on past much of the Namibian coast as far as the twenty-second parallel. With food and water running dangerously low and few places to replenish ashore, it became clear that the voyage could not go on. Faced with the inevitable, Cão went ashore at Cape Cross near today's Walvis Bay, erected his final marker, and gave orders to set a course north. It must have been a crushing personal disappointment, but with the coast stretching endlessly onward, there simply was no way the mission could continue.

On the return trip, Cão halted at the Zaire River once more, this time to visit the manicongo himself. The ship sailed upriver as far as Ielala Falls, where the rapids ruled out any further passage. From there, he set out overland with a few men to the king's capital at Ambasse. Cão, of course, had found out from his men what to expect, as had the manicongo from the four men who had been taken to Portugal. The meeting proceeded cordially, with the manicongo expressing a strong desire to be baptized and to be allied with the king of Portugal. He selected one of the four men to be his ambassador to the Portuguese court and requested priests to teach his people Christianity, as well as others to instruct them in farming and other skills that would improve their lives. "The kingdom of the Congo shall be like Portugal in Africa," he concluded.

Cape Cross, Namibia. A stone marker (padrão) marks the farthest spot reached by Cão and his men.

This was a major achievement, providing Portugal a distinct opportunity to obtain a major ally in tropical Africa, but Cão returned discouraged. Though he had single-handedly added more than fifteen hundred miles of coast to the map of Africa, he had failed to achieve his major objective. Of his reception in Lisbon we know nothing. Barros wrote that Cão met with the king, but some historians suggested that he died on the return trip, never making it back to Portugal. Others speculate that he fell into disfavor for failing to discover the sea link between the Atlantic and Indian oceans. His fate will probably never be known. From the moment Cão left the Zaire, he simply vanishes from most records.

Though Cão or Pêro de Escobar must have briefed the king in detail on the apparently infinite extent of the African coast, John II was not deterred. In fact, he was more determined than ever. Information obtained from a mission to the kingdom of Benin seemed to indicate that the land of the mysterious Prester John was closer than expected. From that, according to Barros, John deduced that the southern tip of Africa couldn't be much beyond Cão's last marker.

So having thought over all these points which gave him an even stronger desire to discover India, he decided to send out later in 1486 two ships by sea and an expedition by land to check on these things which gave him so much hope. Two ships of up to fifty tons each were made ready, as well as a smaller ship to carry extra provisions, because very often on these long voyages the ships ran short of supplies and had to return to the kingdom. They left in late August of that year.

Bartolomeu Dias, Royal Courtier, was given command of the voyage. He already knew part of that coast. The ship he sailed in was piloted by Pero d'Alenquer and Leião was the Master.

The Captain of the second vessel was João Infante while Alvaro Martins was Pilot and João Grego Master. The Captain of the supply ship was Pero Dias, Bartolomeu's brother, its Pilot was João de Santiago and Master João Alves. Each of these officers was an expert in his field.

Bartolomeu Dias's small fleet sailed along the majestic Namib desert. But adverse winds made further progress difficult.

Dias's instructions left no doubt about what was to be achieved this time: to determine once and for all whether there was a sea passage to the Indies.

The small fleet left Lisbon in August 1487 on a voyage that, according to Barros, would last sixteen months and seventeen days. As usual, the ships first called at São Jorge da Mina to provision before pressing on towards Cão's last marker in Namibia. By December the fleet had passed it and sailed as far as the twenty-ninth parallel in southwest Africa. But their further progress became impossible. The winds were blowing so hard from the southwest that even the lateen-rigged caravels hardly made headway.

At first Dias wanted to wait it out, but the weather didn't improve. He then decided to head out into open seas, leaving the cumbersome supply ship behind. It was a courageous move, as Barros made clear:

When he finally left the bad weather continued and he had to sail for thirteen days with sails at half mast. The boats were small and the seas were getting colder, not at all like the Gulf of Guinea. The seas around the Spanish coast were very rough in stormy weather but these were fatal. Then the weather which created so much fury in the sea abated and they started to look for land by turning east. They thought that the coast still ran north-south. However, after a few days they still had not sighted land and they turned north and they came to a bay which they called Vaqueiros because of the many cows they saw there guarded by their cowherds.

"They came to a bay which they called Vaqueiros . . ." Part of Mossel Bay remains undeveloped, giving us an idea of Dias's first view of the South African coast.

They did not understand the language and so communication was impossible. The natives were afraid and herded their animals inland and the only thing our men learned was that they were Negroes with short curly hair like those in Guinea. They followed the coast in a new direction, which made the captains very pleased, and they came to an island lying at 33.75 south. Here they set up a Pillar dedicated to the Cross, which gave the island its name.

Dias and his men had good reason to be pleased. The coast indeed ran in a new direction: first east, then northeast. It seemed they had finally rounded the southern tip of Africa. According to Barros, Dias wanted to move on, but his crew objected:

> The men were very tired and still suffering from the effects of the tempestuous seas they had sailed through. They began to complain and asked not to continue saying that provisions were running out and that they should return to the supply ship and that the further they went on, the greater would be the distance to sail back to the extra supplies and that they would all die of hunger. They said that they had already discovered a lot of new coast and that the greatest news they had was that they thought the land ran generally eastwards and that behind them lay a large cape and that it would be wiser to go back and explore it.

In order to respond to the complaints of so many men, Bartolomeu Dias went ashore with the captains and officers and some of the higher ranking sailors. He made them swear and ordered them under oath to tell the truth about what they thought they should do for the service of the king. They all agreed that

Mossel Bay, South Africa, is the site of the first European landfall in South Africa. Near the waterfront is a statue of Bartolomeu Dias, who discovered the bay in early 1488.

they should return to the kingdom and gave the same reasons as above and others.

Afterwards he ordered that a declaration should be written out and they all signed it. He himself wanted to continue because his sole wish was to fulfil his duty and respect the King's orders. The King had told him to discuss all the important matters with the officers and so, when he saw them signing the declaration, he asked them all to sail along the coast for two or three more days and if they found nothing worthy of interest they would turn back. This was agreed. They sailed on for some time and only arrived at a river which is twenty-five leagues beyond the Cross Island at 32.66 S. The first man to land was João Infante, Captain of the Panteleão and the river was named after him.

Here the men began to repeat their complaints and they turned to Cross Island where Bartolomeu Dias had set up the pillar.

He was filled with such sorrow that it was as if he was leaving and losing a son forever and he remembered the dangers they had all faced and how far they had come to achieve nothing more because God had not granted the main thing. When they left that place they saw that great and noble cape which had stood there for so many years and it seemed to promise a new world of lands. Bartolomeu Dias and his men named it Cape of Storms because of the dangers and storms they had suffered on rounding it.

However, when they returned to the kingdom, King John gave it another name. He called it the Cape of Good Hope because it promised the long awaited discovery of India.

How much of this is true is hard to say. Writing early in the sixteenth century, Duarte Pacheco Pereira, an experienced navigator, explains that Dias himself called it the Cape of Good Hope. Pereira should have known, because Dias took him from the island of Principe on his return trip from the cape. But Barros's version sound more romantic, with the hardy navigator recollecting the experience of rounding the cape in stormy seas in a small caravel, and his king later renaming it. Good Hope because nearly seventy-five years after their first conquest in Africa the Portuguese had finally rounded its southernmost point. Good Hope, for now the riches of the East were finally in sight.

It would be many years before Vasco da Gama set out to claim these riches, which may seem surprising for a king who was so eager to reach India. But they weren't wasted years. A lot had to be done before the voyage to India could be considered a feasible proposition.

It is a tribute to John's farsightedness that he realized this and suppressed the urge to dispatch an expedition immediately. Instead he proceeded methodically, as if ticking off a checklist. First on the list was the consolidation of his position in Africa. Trade with the continent had grown very profitable, but controlling it demanded constant attention. There also was the continuing desire to spread Christianity, an effort to salvage the millions of lost souls awaiting word of the "true faith." Finally, John realized that he needed allies. There was no question that a voyage to the Indies would be long and difficult, creating the need for strategically placed provisioning ports. El Mina was one, and it proved convenient, but more were needed.

The Cape of Good Hope. According to legend, Dias first called it the Cape of Storms, because of the difficulties experienced in rounding it.

Given the distance from Portugal to Central and South Africa, much of the country's consolidation efforts initially focused on West Africa. The uninhabited Cape Verde Islands, sighted by Cadamosto in the mid 1450s, were colonized in the early 1460s, after Antonio da Noli had established himself as the first governor on the island of Santiago. With few natural resources of their own, life proved difficult at first, but it didn't take long for the settlers to divert slaves from the mainland to work the fields.

Inspired by the success of Madeira, the settlers wanted to grow sugar cane, but neither the soil nor the climate cooperated. In fact, there wasn't a great deal that prospered in the island's dry climate, forcing the immigrants to look for other ways of making a living. One materialized in the 1470s when it became clear that the islands provided a convenient steppingstone to the riches of Africa. Ships began to call at the port of Ribeiro Grande on Santiago to provision on their way to and from the West African coast.

With Ribeiro Grande, Portugal obtained a new base. The trading post at Arguin was still in operation, but was no more than a place to exchange goods, rapidly losing its importance because of the discoveries farther south. Ribeiro Grande proved far more convenient, with plenty of deep water, a relatively well-protected anchorage, and better access to the Guinean trade. It also had a *ribeiro*—a pool of fresh water which hardly ever dried up. More people began to settle there, giving Portugal its first major base in West Africa.

Due east along the mainland was Senegal, where trade had been conducted for many years though no major alliances had been established. It was good news therefore when Bemoin, a chief of the kingdom of Jalofa, sought Portuguese protection after having been deposed by a rival in 1487.

From Arguin, Bemoin was taken to Lisbon, where he soon expressed a wish to be baptized. The opportunity to have a strong Christian ally in West Africa was too good to pass up, and Bemoin was baptized with King John and Queen Leonor at his side. Not long thereafter a powerful fleet was assembled to return Bemoin to Senegal and make sure he regained the throne. Once that had taken place, the men aboard, led by Pêro Vaz da Cunha, were to construct a fortress at the mouth of the Senegal River.

Unfortunately nothing ever came of these plans because Cunha had Bemoin executed on the trip south, for what remain obscure reasons. The fleet returned to Lisbon the same year, the prefabricated fortress still in the ships' holds. No further attempts were made to establish a stronger foothold in the Senegal region, though trade continued for many years.

Further east, the fortress at El Mina had become a profitable trading post, but it was a poor base for inland exploration. Local chiefs were eager to trade, but they resisted inland excursions, fearing that it might cause them to lose control of that trade. Even so, a Portuguese delegation made it to Gao, capital of the powerful Songhai empire. But the trip proved futile, because Songhai's Muslim ruler wasn't interested in a Portuguese alliance and certainly wouldn't let Portugese missionaries preach the blessings of Christianity.

Muslim rulers made prospects equally uncertain in the kingdom of

Benin, which covered modern Benin and much of Nigeria. Nevertheless, a mission was sent there between 1484 and 1486, headed by João Afonso de Aveiro. Despite the religious differences, Aveiro succeeded in establishing relations with the king of Benin. Portuguese merchants soon followed, exchanging European goods for slaves, who were in turn carried on to El Mina, where they were traded for gold. The Portuguese also

The beach at São Tomé, capital of the republic of São Tomé e Principe. The Portuguese began to colonize the island in the 1490s.

obtained malaguetta pepper from the region, which fetched high prices in Lisbon and the rest of Europe.

Given the promising trade prospects in Benin, John II ordered the establishment of a factory in Gwato, at the western end of the Niger delta. It was built, but so many Portuguese died as a result of the unhealthy living conditions that it had to be abandoned. Instead, the Portuguese stationed agents at the capital city of Benin, maintaining trading links and cordial relations between the two kingdoms for more than a century.

At roughly the same time, the Portuguese also began to explore the possibilities of the island of São Tomé. Found uninhabited during the early 1470s, it remained untouched and unexplored at first, but during the late 1480s and 1490s the Portuguese began to colonize it, sending convicts along with Jewish children, exiled so that they wouldn't practice their religion. Many succumbed to tropical diseases, but São Tomé's colonization succeeded as a result of the captaincy of Alvaro de

São Tomé still contains plenty of remnants of its Portuguese roots.

Caminha. It was Caminha who introduced sugar cane to the island which, thanks to the ideal climate and soil, quickly developed into a profitable crop. And it was Caminha who introduced the manpower to work the fields, diverting thousands of slaves from the mainland to the island. Many of them subsequently obtained their freedom, but at the expense of tens of thousands of others, for what was practiced on a small scale in São Tomé would soon be applied on a much larger scale across the Atlantic in Brazil.

The combination of the ideal climate and slave labor made sugar cane São Tomé's principal crop.

With Arguin, Cabo Verde, El Mina, and São Tomé, the Portuguese had several strategically placed bases, although few allies. But Diogo Cão's initial forays in the Congo would help change that.

Three years after Cão's return, King John sent a fleet of ships headed by Gonçalo de Sousa to the Congo. Aboard, aside from sailors and soldiers, were the missionaries, farmers, and artisans the manicongo had requested. But the trip south proved difficult, with Sousa and a Congolese envoy dying of the plague along the way. It took four months for the fleet to reach the Zaire River.

Once there, the mission proceeded more smoothly. Contacts were reestablished with the local population, and before long the missionaries were busy converting thousands of natives in the region. The Portuguese received an even warmer reception from the manicongo at his capital of Ambasse. A few days later he was baptized, along with thousands of his subjects. In honor of the king and queen of Portugal, the manicongo was christened Dom João de Congo while his wife became Dona Leonor. That same day the foundations of a church were laid and Ambasse was renamed São Salvador. To seal the alliance, some Portuguese joined an expedition against rebellious tribesmen, helping the manicongo win a resounding victory.

This promising start seemed to provide John II with his long-sought African ally, though there was some internal opposition at first. One of the manicongo's sons was baptized and named Afonso, after John II's own son, but another took a dim view of Christianity. It didn't take him long to find people who shared his view, and they began plotting a return to the old way of doing things. After a while, even the manicongo grew disenchanted, especially after being reminded time after time by the Portuguese friars that he was limited to one wife. So did the displaced royal wives, who were about to lose a great deal of power and prestige. They joined the plotters in opposition to Christianity.

When the manicongo died, the stage was set for a classic power struggle, pitting the Christian forces loyal to Afonso against those of his brother. Though Afonso was heavily outnumbered, this wasn't anything that a few miracles couldn't solve. According to contemporary chroniclers, a mysterious rain of arrows fell on the unbelievers as soon as they entered the city, while the Christian forces remained unharmed. Calling on God and St. James, they thoroughly routed their opponents, many of whom decided to switch sides on the spot, convinced that this new god was far more powerful than anything they had ever known.

Thus began a period of cordial relations between the two nations, with Portugal exerting a good deal of influence in the region. The priests who stayed behind continued their missionary work, bringing about the first phase of "making Congo like Portugal in Africa." The artisans, too, contributed to Congolese life, teaching farming methods as well as carpentry and other trades. A few Portuguese stayed in the Congo with specific orders to venture inland and "discover other diverse lands." Aided by native guides they proceeded, though it remains unclear how far they actually went. Even so, there is little doubt that the first white men in much of tropical Africa were not nineteenth-century explorers but Portuguese adventurers who preceded them by hundreds of years. They collected information about trade and geography that helped Portugal consolidate its position in Equatorial Africa.

Although small and hardly known, São Tomé carries a sad legacy, for it was here that black slave labor proved its value in the farming of tropical crops. Before long, millions of slaves would be carried across the Atlantic to work American fields as well.

Unfortunately, this state of relative harmony wouldn't last. During the sixteenth century, after the initial years of Asian euphoria had worn off, more Portuguese started heading for the Congo, among them merchants intent on making a fortune in the slave trade. What they couldn't obtain from African chiefs they began to take themselves, raiding the local population. At one point Congo's King Afonso wrote to the king of Portugal—supposedly his "brother"—pleading for a halt to the continuing drain of his people, but in vain. There was too much money to be made and more people were taken, especially after slaves began to be sent across the Atlantic to work the Brazilian sugar fields. In the spirit of the times they were baptized prior to the trip, but that didn't improve their lot. If anything it only provided the Portuguese some peace of mind, convinced as they were that the saving of lost souls justified the enslavement of their bodies. Under these circumstances, healthy relations between the two kingdoms could not survive.

In spite of such unfortunate developments, at the end of the fifteenth century the situation in Africa looked promising. Trade was growing both in volume and profitability, a number of bases had been established, and Portugal had found an ally in the central part of the continent. From bases, trading posts, and even individual adventurers, information flowed into Portugal, much of it totally new to the West.

These efforts strengthened Portugal's position in West and Central Africa, but there was a need for information about the eastern part of the continent as well. After all, once a ship or fleet rounded the Cape of Good Hope on its way to India, it would have to venture along the East African coast prior to setting out across the Indian Ocean. No one in Europe had any information on this region, though there was a general assumption that Prester John held a great deal of influence there. Reaching him or his realm would solve a good many pieces of the East African puzzle, or so it was believed.

There is little doubt that John's emissaries in West and tropical Africa were requested to find out more about Prester John, but when they failed to come up with any information, the king decided on a more direct approach. In 1484 he dispatched two priests with specific orders to reach the court of Prester John. Traveling openly as envoys of the king of Portugal they made it as far as Jerusalem, but there the mission came to a grinding halt. Beyond were Muslim territories, and the two Christian emissaries were not allowed through.

A few years later John dispatched a second mission, this time with considerably less pomp. He selected Pêro da Covilhã and Afonso de Paiva, darkly tanned villagers who spoke flawless Arabic and were

A small chapel stands near the mouth of the Kwanza river south of Luanda. Here Angolan slaves were baptized prior to being shipped out.

experienced in Muslim customs. Unlike their predecessors they were eminently capable of passing as Arab merchants.

Covilhã and Paiva set out together, traveling to Barcelona from where they set sail to Rhodes. There they caught another ship that took them to Alexandria, where they joined a group of merchants for the trip to the Red Sea. Setting out in a dhow, they eventually reached Aden, where they split up. Of Afonso de Paiva's wanderings nothing is known other than that he died on the way to the court of Prester John. Covilhã, on the other hand, left a trail which clearly identifies him as one of Portugal's greatest, though least recognized, travelers.

In Aden, according to Barros, Covilhã secured passage aboard a dhow bound for India. Although we don't have many details of his wanderings there, he apparently spent more than a year along the Indian west coast, traveling to Cananor, Calicut, and Goa. Along the way he collected information not only about trade but also about the political and military situation, presumably with an eye to making suggestions as to where the first Portuguese fleet to venture that way should head.

When his task in India was completed, Covilhã set out for Hormuz, the great trading port at the entrance to the Persian Gulf. Once it had been thoroughly scouted, he shipped out again, this time down the East African coast as far as Sofala in today's Mozambique, where Arab merchants traded their products for gold from the African interior. Few details of his travels down the East African coast have survived, but there is no question that Covilhã collected valuable intelligence on the region. After calling at a number of trading centers north of Sofala, he finally reached Aden again, from where he made his way to Cairo.

By the time Covilhã arrived there, he had been on the road for more than three years, but his travels weren't over yet. In the Egyptian capital he was met by two Jewish agents of John II, who gave him a new set of instructions. Since Paiva had failed to reach the court of Prester John, he was to make his way there, to establish an alliance with the current ruler.

Before setting out once more, Covilhã recounted his travels to the agents, then wrote a detailed report. Unfortunately the report probably never made it to Lisbon or, if it did, it was never shown to the people who needed to see it. Sending Covilhã to the court of Prester John in Ethiopia thus proved to be one of John II's few mistakes, for he never heard from Covilhã firsthand. Neither did any of his chroniclers. "He never returned from his travels," one of them wrote, assuming that Covilhã died on the way.

But Covilhã *did* make it to Ethiopia, by way of Aden and Hormuz. When Portugal sent a mission to the court of Prester John thirty years later, they found Covilhã alive and well. Having been prevented from leaving for all that time, he had settled there, married, and fathered several children. But Covilhã was now too old to make the long trip to his homeland. One of Portugal's most courageous and resourceful travelers, he died a few years afterwards.

With Covilhã reconnoitering India, Bartolomeu Dias proving there was a sea passage to the Indies, and merchants and missionaries consolidating Portugal's position in Africa, the time seemed ripe to finally plan a voyage to the Indies. But there were two major difficulties that remained to be resolved: one foreseen, the other not.

Dias's and Cão's trips along the African coast had made clear that whomever was sent to India would face an extremely long and dangerous journey. In fact, the contrary winds and currents encountered along southwest Africa suggested that unless an alternate route could be found, it might not even prove practical for cargo ships. After all, Dias had been forced to leave his supply ship behind. There was simply no way a square-rigged ship could have progressed against the prevailing winds and currents.

Finding an alternate route required additional information about wind and current conditions in the South Atlantic, which meant that someone had to go there. There are some good arguments supporting the notion that another voyage, or set of voyages, was dispatched to the South Atlantic, but no evidence. No records survive, either because they were suppressed or destroyed.

Whoever went probably investigated the possibility of avoiding the adverse conditions by making a wide detour into the South Atlantic, much the same way Portuguese sailors did in the northern hemisphere on their return from the Gulf of Guinea. That strategy took Dias around the Cape, and it would later allow Vasco da Gama to reach the Cape as well. But while Dias's detour began far down the Namibian coast, Vasco da Gama headed out much sooner, thereby staying out of sight of land for three months. There is no way that he could or would have done this without advance knowledge, suggesting that someone paved the way. It is tempting to speculate who might have done so: Dias perhaps, or Duarte Pacheco Pereira, whom Dias had picked up on his homebound voyage. In fact, Portugal had no shortage of extremely capable mariners. One or more of Vasco da Gama's pilots might have been along for the trip as well, though none of them ever mentioned it in subsequent accounts.

The speculation doesn't end there. Some sailors may even have sighted or reached South America by following the South Atlantic trade winds for too long. When Cabral did so on his way to the Indies in 1500, officially "discovering" Brazil in the process, the report sent back to Portugal doesn't express a great deal of surprise. Its matter-of-fact style seems to indicate that people already knew of its existence. But of this no one is certain. In fact, much of Portugal's navigational activities between 1488 and 1497, especially in the western reaches of the Atlantic, remain shrouded in mystery. The Portuguese of the fifteenth century were arguably the world's most daring explorers, constantly extending the borders of the unknown. But they kept the exact extent of what they knew hidden, even from their own chroniclers.

Even with a feasible route charted through the South Atlantic, an unforeseen difficulty remained to be dealt with before the first voyage to India could proceed.

Dias's return from the Cape of Good Hope in late 1488 was witnessed by a man who was sorely disappointed by its implications. He had spent a great deal of time in Portugal, trying to convince King John II and others that the best way to reach the Indies was not to go south around Africa and thence east, but rather to sail west into the Atlantic. His name was Christopher Columbus.

Columbus's Portuguese connections are well-established. He probably arrived in the mid-1470s—according to one story, the victim of a shipwreck—and looked up his younger brother, who worked as a chartmaker in Lisbon. From that time he moved ahead rapidly. Perhaps it was the result of his Genoese connections; others feel it may have had something to do with obscure family ties. At any rate, before long Columbus moved in the highest mercantile circles. He even managed an entry into Portuguese aristocracy by marrying Filipa Perestrelo, the daughter of one of the first captains of Porto Santo.

As a result of his marriage, Columbus traveled frequently between Madeira, the Azores, and Portugal during the late 1470s and early 1480s and made at least one trip to the Portuguese fortress at El Mina. He became an experienced mariner in the process, benefiting greatly from Portugal's pool of knowledge about winds and currents in the Atlantic. It was also during that time that he found out about the islands that were believed to exist west of the Azores. Some of the evidence was flimsy, culled from a variety of sailor's tales. Some of it was based on actual reports by mariners blown off course who claimed to have sighted land but could not locate it on subsequent trips. And some of the evidence seemed to be solid: plants and other debris washing ashore in the Azores, for instance, or the flight paths of birds seen heading west in the middle of the Atlantic.

Like many others, Columbus became convinced there was land across the Atlantic, but he went one step further: he identified it. In his view this wasn't just some unknown or mythical land mass; it was nothing less than Asia. To back up these conclusions, Columbus made some calculations, but they were far off the mark. For one thing, he underestimated the circumference of the earth, thus reducing the size of the oceans. For another, he overestimated the size of the Eurasian continent. Combined, these two miscalculations brought the eastern fringe of Asia much closer to Europe than it actually is. In Columbus's view, the two were separated by no more than a few thousand miles.

It is generally believed that Columbus began to collect evidence for his transatlantic plans during the early 1480s. Next he needed to garner support for the enterprise. In Portugal that demanded a royal blessing. No one set sail to discover new lands without the king's approval.

In 1483 Columbus was granted an audience with John II. But he didn't merely ask for the king's blessing. He wanted the king to finance the expedition, making three vessels and their crews available to sail under his command. In return, he asserted, Portugal would gain vast new territories as well as untold wealth.

This wasn't the first time John II received a proposal of this nature, but it differed in two important respects. For one thing, there were the demands, which struck everyone at the court as preposterous. The king had given previous applicants permission to sail west, but always on the condition that they financed the voyages themselves. For another, there was the issue of identification. Previous applicants went in search of unknown lands or, at best, the near-mythical island of the Seven Cities. Columbus was guaranteeing that he would reach Asia.

Despite Columbus's relative lack of experience, his proposal was carefully examined by a committee that reviewed all matters pertaining to overseas exploration. It included cartographers, mathematicians and astronomers, like José Vizinho, who would later sail with Diogo Cão, as well as Duarte Pacheco Pereira. Diogo Ortiz de Vilhegas, the king's doctor, turned in the verdict. The committee didn't necessarily disagree with the notion that there was land to the west, but it ruled out that it was Asia.

King John concurred. Though he had been intrigued by Columbus's proposal, he knew Portugal didn't need a foreign upstart to go check what was on the other side of the Atlantic. Besides, he couldn't afford to spend resources on two fronts. With Diogo Cão recently returned from his first voyage and implying that the passage to the Indies was near, John felt the African option was a safer bet.

Dejected, Columbus made his way to Spain. His efforts had put him deeply in debt, and it probably wasn't a good idea for him to stay in Portugal. He may also have wanted to take his plan to Ferdinand and Isabella, who had recently unified the kingdoms of Aragon and Castile. Perhaps they would be more open to the idea.

Unfortunately, *Los Reyes Católicos* had many other things on their minds, including the conquest of Granada. As a result, Columbus spent many frustrating years in Spain. In 1488 he returned briefly to Portugal, possibly at the invitation of King John. Cão's failure to find a sea passage to the Indies may have rekindled interest in the transatlantic option. But when he witnessed the return of Dias's voyage, Columbus must have known it marked the end of any possibilities in Portugal and soon returned to Spain.

It would take several more years to convince Ferdinand and Isabella, but after Granada had been conquered in early 1492, Columbus finally got the royal go-ahead, along with the ships and titles he demanded. After waiting all those years to prove his theories, Columbus lost no time. He left from Palos in southwestern Spain in August of the same year.

Seven months later, in early March 1493, Columbus returned from his first voyage, sailing into the Tagus river on his way to Lisbon. Perhaps he merely wanted to inform John II of his discovery, but there undoubtedly was a desire to even the score as well. During a meeting at the court, Columbus acted confidently and almost arrogantly, chiding the king for failing to support him several years earlier. According to royal chronicler Rui de Pina, the explorer accused the king of "being gloomy because he had refused him through lack of credit and authority . . . the first time he had made his request."

Gloomy or not, John II was most interested in Columbus' reports. Not because he thought Columbus had reached Asia; neither the few natives Columbus had brought along nor their meager belongings looked Asian. No, the king was interested because he wanted to make sure the navigator hadn't trespassed into Portuguese waters. After all, the Treaty of Alcáçovas, which John had helped negotiate in 1479, stipulated that any lands south of the Canary islands, "discovered and to be discovered," belonged to Portugal. The clause in question admittedly mentioned Guinea, implying the Portuguese were probably referring to discoveries in the vicinity of Africa. But it could also be interpreted to include any lands south of a parallel running through the Canaries. If Columbus's new-found islands lay south of the demarcation line, they would thus belong to Portugal. As far as John was concerned, the distance from Guinea was irrelevant.

Although seemingly greedy, this position was not simply pulled out of a hat. On several previous occasions John II had let it be known that any lands beyond the Canary Islands "will belong to us and our kingdoms and successors forever." No one objected at the time, but Columbus's discovery created complications. Ferdinand and Isabella weren't going to let the fruits of their investment pass into Portuguese hands.

To shift the momentum John took action. Less than a month after meeting with Columbus he convened his council and decided to send a heavily armed fleet west, with the obvious intent of claiming the newly discovered western islands for Portugal. When Ferdinand and Isabella found out about the plan, they immediately dispatched a messenger to Lisbon. He delivered an urgent request to postpone any action "until it was decided by law who the said seas and conquests belonged to."

That request would lead to negotiations for one of the most interesting and presumptuous treaties between two countries. At first there was some additional maneuvering by both sides, with the Spanish monarchs in particular moving rapidly to consolidate their position. They quickly approved Columbus's second voyage, hoping to solidify their claim to the West Indies, and petitioned the Pope for a ruling on the issue.

Since the conversion of the inhabitants of any newly discovered lands was, at least in theory, one of the principal goals of exploration, papal rulings were very significant. John II never hesitated to back up his claims with papal bulls, but this time he had no luck. The occupant of the Vatican at the time was Alexander VI, the most notorious member of the Spanish Borgia family to hold the office. With few if any religious credentials, Alexander had relied heavily on the support of Ferdinand and Isabella to get elected, and now he was asked to return the favor. He did exactly as told.

Early in May 1493, barely two months after Columbus's return, Alexander VI issued a series of papal bulls, the most important of which divided the world into two parts by a meridian—a line drawn from north to south—one hundred miles west of the Azores or Cape Verde Islands. All lands discovered or yet to be discovered east of the line would belong to Portugal, all territories to the west of it to Spain.

The Portuguese at first tried to ignore the papal decisions, hoping to buy more time, but that proved difficult. Regardless of the credentials of the Vatican's occupant, pontifical decisions were not easily ignored. So John II sent a messenger to the Spanish court, requesting in turn that no voyages be sent west until the dispute had been resolved and cautioning that anything to the contrary could damage relations between the two countries. His demands fell on deaf ears. Ferdinand and Isabella knew they had the Vatican on their side and that there was little Portugal could do. They sent Columbus on a second voyage in September 1493.

Though John continued to insist on the dividing line of the Treaty of Alcáçovas, he began to realize that he couldn't win this one. He therefore shifted his strategy, officially insisting on the parallel dividing line but preparing to settle for a meridian. But John didn't want the line the pope had set; he wanted it moved further west. The only way he was going to achieve that was by acting as if he were making a concession; not the other way around.

When final negotiations began in early 1494, the Portuguese accordingly demanded that the line established by Alexander VI be moved 270 leagues (950 miles) further west, from 100 leagues west of the Cape Verde Islands to 370 leagues—a difference of fourteen degrees of longitude. Everyone realized that this was a great distance, and negotiations must have been extremely tedious. But John II never wavered, agreeing only to the stipulation that if before July 1494 any lands were discovered within the most westerly 120 leagues of the Portuguese zone, they would belong to Spain. Columbus was still off on his second voyage at the time, and Ferdinand and Isabella apparently wanted to safeguard any new discoveries.

As it turned out, Columbus never found any land within that zone, though it existed farther south. The easternmost part of Brazil penetrated deep into the Portuguese zone, though no one was supposed to know that. While it doesn't conclusively prove that the Portuguese already knew of the existence of Brazil, it does raise interesting questions. With some of their mariners exploring wind and current patterns in the South Atlantic at that time, it is possible, and in the view of some historians even probable, that one of them landed on, or at least sighted, the South American continent.

However, there is no proof. Aside from the matter-of-fact mention of the official "discovery" of Brazil and other vague references, there is no evidence to indicate that Portugal knew of or had any designs on Brazil. It is possible, for instance, that the Portuguese simply wanted to deny the area to the Spanish. By then they knew that the voyage to India would require a long detour into the South Atlantic, and they might have wanted to insure that their mariners would be able to do so unhindered.

The agreement dividing the world between Portugal and Spain was concluded on June 7, 1494, in Tordesillas, Spain. Ferdinand and Isabella signed it two days later; John II took more time, not ratifying it until early September. With it, Portugal was granted large territories in Africa, Asia, and Brazil. Spain, on the other hand, received control over most of the Americas, though many in Castile still thought Columbus had reached the easternmost fringe of Asia.

By the time the Portuguese king signed the Treaty of Tordesillas, he was very ill. For several years a mysterious illness had afflicted him, growing progressively worse. Though not yet forty, his hair and beard had turned white, his hands were swollen, and sometimes he could hardly move. So far as he was able, John continued to behave as if he were healthy, but he apparently realized that he was mortally ill. A year later, on October 25, he died at Alvor near Lagos. He had come to the Algarve hoping the springs at Monchique would restore his health. In the end, the long trip probably killed him.

Like his great-uncle, John II was buried in Batalha, not far from where Henry and the other members of the "noble generation" rest. It is fitting. John, more than anyone else, prepared the path to the Indies. It was said of Bartolomeu Dias that he "saw the land of India but did not enter it, like Moses and the Promised Land." It applies to John II as well. His tireless efforts brought the Promised Land finally within reach.

CHAPTER 3

The Passage to India

Now land was close at hand,
the land so many had longed to reach,
that lay between the Ganges and the Indus.
Go forward, brave men, you have arrived.
Ahead is the land of wealth abounding.

Luís de Camões
The Lusiads, Canto VII

In the name of God. Amen!

In the year 1497 King Dom Manuel, the first of that name in Portugal, dispatched four vessels to make discoveries and go in search of spices. Vasco da Gama was the captain-major of these vessels; Paulo da Gama, his brother, commanded one of them, and Nicolau Coelho another.

We left Restello on Saturday, July 8, 1497. May God our Lord permit us to accomplish this voyage in his service.

Amen!

*t*hus begins the one surviving eyewitness account of one of the most important voyages in the history of the world.

It was kept as a diary by someone who couldn't possibly have imagined its future importance. Though it wasn't signed, simple elimination leads us to the name of Álvaro Velho, probably a soldier aboard one of the ships. No doubt there were other reports and accounts, most of them presumably a great deal more "official," but they have vanished. Velho's account is the only one left, making it invaluable.

Velho wasn't one to waste many words on simple things. "We left Restello on Saturday, July 8, 1497," he wrote, dismising a scene that begs for more. Later renderings take up the slack, weaving a moving story around the departure of the fleet, with wives, mothers, and children seeing their husbands, sons, and fathers off on what many, no doubt, believed was a one-way trip.

The Lusiads, Portugal's national epic poem, paints a somber picture of the departure, even though Camões wrote many years afterwards and thus already knew the voyage's outcome. His opening scene is peopled with grieving mothers, saddened wives, and old men who shake their heads when they see the men pass on their way to the ships. There is a sense of impending doom, of vainglory and lust for wealth certain to lead to disaster. "Would it not have been far more tolerable to be carried off by any kind of death onshore, rather than to be buried in the waves so far from home?" another chronicler wrote. He voiced the opinion of many who saw the men off on that July morning five hundred years ago.

Though Velho and his colleagues presumably felt more confident, even high officials had their doubts. In 1495, shortly after the death of John II, the newly crowned King Manuel had summoned his council to discuss whether Portugal should go ahead with a voyage to India. The majority were opposed. They pointed to the incalculable risks and costs, the many dangers and uncertainties, and the jealousies that would be aroused in other countries if the voyage were successful. But Manuel held a different view. "I have inherited from my predecessors a sacred mission," he said. "Their labors must not be brought to naught. I am prepared to leave these matters in the hands of God, in the conviction that He, of His great goodness, will find a way to bring profit to the Kingdom".

These were strong words for someone who had inherited the throne just a few month earlier and had, until then, been hardly noticed. But Manuel often acted as if he had been chosen for a special task, resorting to lofty words to underscore that belief. Perhaps he had a point, because his path to the kingship seemed fateful.

King John's son Afonso, who would normally have inherited the throne, had died in a riding accident in 1490. Next in line would have been Diogo, John II's cousin, but he had been implicated in a plot to overthrow the king and had been stabbed to death by John himself. Manuel was Diogo's younger brother and thus third in line, but John also had an illegitimate son whom he tried to get on the throne during the last year of his life. For that to happen, the bastard son had to be declared legitimate, which required the support of his family as well as approval by the pope. Neither materialized. Though the queen was reportedly friendly to the young man, she saw no need to support the offspring of her husband's affair. The pope also refused to endorse the lineage, on the advice of the Spanish monarchs and others who preferred Manuel. Faced with the inevitable, John named his cousin heir to the throne. But Manuel didn't repay the favor. He didn't even bother to show up when the dying king summoned him to the Algarve.

Manuel was twenty-six when he ascended the throne a few days after John's death and, although he differed in many respects from his predecessor, he clearly was intrigued by the prospect of reaching the Indies. Despite the opinion of his council, he ordered the voyage to proceed, placing the experienced Bartolomeu Dias in charge of its preparations.

Dias would have been a suitable choice to head the expedition, but in early 1497 Manuel appointed Vasco da Gama instead. According to João de Barros the appointment came by right, having been offered to his late father by King John a few years earlier. Another account is less specific, noting that Manuel offered the captaincy upon meeting Gama at the court.

Both versions are doubtful, because the expedition's leadership was unquestionably one of the most important appointments in Portugal. One would have expected someone very experienced in seamanship or diplomacy, preferably both, but Gama was neither. Having grown up in the fishing port of Sines where his father was civil governor, he was familiar with the ways of the sea but had never undertaken a major voyage. Gama obtained a solid education in Evora, but hadn't been trained in policy or diplomacy. In the end, Vasco da Gama proved himself to be a solid leader and possibly the best choice for the task, but the reasons for his appointment remain obscure. There must have been something that impressed King Manuel, especially since so many of his advisors didn't believe the voyage should proceed at all.

By the spring of 1497 the fleet was taking shape. Two ships—the *São Gabriel* and *São Rafael*—had been specifically built for the voyage. Square-rigged on both the foremast and the main mast, they were larger than the caravels that had been sent out up to this point, presumably because they were expected to bring back a cargo. They also carried twenty guns apiece. Accompanying the carracks was the *São Miguel*, a caravel better known as the *Bérrio* after its previous owner. And rounding out the fleet was a large unnamed supply ship, stowed with three years' worth of food and supplies. Distributed in the other vessels were trading goods: cloth, caps, glass beads, copper bowls, little bells, and a variety of other trinkets, to be handed out along the way. These had been successful in West Africa but would become a liability in the more sophisticated regions of East Africa and India. Of course, the Portuguese didn't know that. They had only a vague idea of what to expect once they entered unknown waters.

The *São Gabriel* was commanded by Gama and piloted by Pêro de Alenquer, who had sailed with Dias to the Cape of Good Hope. The *São Rafael* was captained by Gama's older brother Paulo, who took João de Coimbra as his pilot. And the *Bérrio* was led by Nicolau Coelho and piloted by Pêro de Escobar, a veteran of several expeditions. In all, the fleet carried some 150 people, among them sailors and soldiers, secretaries and interpreters, and a number of *degredados*—convicts who had been offered their freedom in exchange for performing the most dangerous tasks.

As Velho indicates, the fleet left Restello near Lisbon on the morning of July 8, 1497. Unfortunately, he doesn't have a great deal to say about the first part of the trip, briefly describing how the ships sailed through the Canaries and made for Santiago in the Cape Verde Islands, which they reached two weeks after leaving Lisbon. There the fleet spent some time repairing the rigging and provisioning. It set out in early August. What followed still ranks as a very impressive nautical feat:

> On Thursday, August 3, we left in an easterly direction. On August 18, when about two hundred leagues from Santiago, the captain-major's main yard broke, and we lay to under foresail and lower mainsail for two days. On the 22nd of the same month, when going south by west, we saw many birds resembling herons. On the approach of night they flew vigorously to the southeast, as if making for the land.
>
> On Friday October 27, we saw many whales, as well as dolphins and seals.
>
> On Wednesday November 1, we perceived many indications of the proximity of land, including gulfweed, which grows along the coast.
>
> On Saturday the 4th of the same month, a couple of hours before the break of day, we had soundings in 110 fathoms and at nine o'clock we sighted the land. We then drew near to each other, and having put on our gala clothes, we saluted the captain major by firing our bombards and dressed the ships

St. Helena, South Africa. After three months at sea, Gama's fleet made its first South African landfall here.

with flags and standards. In the course of the day we tacked so as to come close to the land, but as we failed to identify it, we again stood out to sea.

The ships stayed out for another three days before approaching land again, finding a sheltered bay with plenty of water. Here the crews anchored and went ashore.

According to Barros, Gama's pilots took latitude measurements, confirming that they were no more than thirty leagues north of the Cape of Good Hope. Considering that the fleet had been at sea for three months without a single landmark, with neither charts nor tables of winds and currents, and without the means to measure longitude, this was an astounding navigational achievement. In the annals of maritime exploration, it was nothing short of a triumph.

The profile of Table Mountain made clear that they were nearing the Cape. Soon it would become a welcome landmark for all sailors heading to the East.

We don't know why Velho doesn't have more to say about this feat. Perhaps he hadn't been feeling well for the three months the fleet was out at sea or, being a soldier, he didn't appreciate it. Or maybe the information was deliberately suppressed by later censors. The Portuguese didn't want to broadcast their navigational methods to the rest of Europe.

The men spent eight days in the region, calling their anchorage St. Helena's Bay—the name it bears to this day. Aside from cleaning the ships and provisioning, they encountered other people for the first time in more than three months. According to Velho, the interaction with the local Hottentots at first proceeded cordially, even though neither side understood the other. The Portuguese presented trinkets like bells and beads but quickly discovered that there wasn't much to be traded. When the ships had stocked up on water and other supplies, the decision was made to head on for the Cape of Good Hope.

Two days later, on November 18, 1497, the cape was sighted. Rounding it was another matter. Contrary winds ruled out much progress, and it took nearly a week before the fleet finally managed to sail beyond it. A day or so later, the ships reached Mossel Bay, which Pêro de Alenquer recognized as Dias's first South African landfall.

The fleet spent thirteen days here, transferring the supplies from the supply ship to the other vessels. The slow and cumbersome ship was then burned. Much of the activity was observed by the Hottentots. Their friendliness surprised Velho because when Dias had landed ten years earlier the natives had fled. Now they were eager to barter, trad-

The Cape of Good Hope. It took nearly a week before Gama's fleet was able to round it.

ing a black ox for three bracelets. "We dined off this ox on Sunday," Velho wrote, adding that the meat was "as toothsome as the beef of Portugal." The Hottentots also danced and played flutes, "making a pretty harmony for Negroes who are not expected to be musicians."

But not all interaction proceeded so cordially. When the Portuguese erected a cross and a pillar on the headland overlooking the bay, the Hottentots appeared less hospitable. "The cross was made out of a mizzen mast and very high," Velho observed. "On the following Thursday, when about to set sail, we saw about ten or twelve Negroes who demolished both the cross and the pillar before we had left." With that, the fleet left Mossel Bay.

One week later the three ships passed the furthest point reached by Bartolomeu Dias. From that point on the Portuguese were in unexplored territory. But it was difficult even to enter it, as Velho recollected:

> On Saturday we passed the last pillar, and as we ran along the coast we observed two men running along the beach in a direction contrary to that which we followed. The country about here is very charming and well wooded; we saw much cattle, and the further we advanced the more did the character of the country improve, and the trees increase in size.
>
> On the next day we sailed along the coast before a stern wind,

when the wind springing round to the east we stood to sea. And thus we kept making tack until sunset on Tuesday, when the wind again veered to the west. We then lay to during the night in order that we might on the following day examine the coast and find out where we were.

In the morning we made straight for the land, and at ten o'clock found ourselves once more at Cross Island, that is sixty leagues abaft our dead reckoning! This was due to the currents, which are very strong here.

That very day we again went forward by the route we had already attempted and being favored during three or four days by a strong stern wind, we were able to overcome the currents which we had feared might frustrate our plans. Henceforth it pleased God in His mercy to allow us to make headway! We were not again driven back. May it please Him that it be thus always!

Gama's fleet made its first East African landfall near today's Inharime, Mozambique.

It was the strong Agulhas current that hindered the fleet's progress. But once the winds turned in their favor the ships made up for the delays. It now was close to Christmas. To commemorate it the Portuguese called the attractive coast they were passing Natal. Shortly thereafter the winds turned again, forcing the fleet to stay farther out to sea. Before long, water supplies began to run low, so a course towards the mainland was set.

The Portuguese landed near a small river in the vicinity of today's Inharime in Mozambique. Here too they encountered people, though not the Hottentots of South Africa. They were back in Bantu territory. The first meeting was congenial, with the local chief providing water and food, including chickens which, according to Velho, were "just like those we have in Portugal." Velho also described the people and their products, houses, and activities. In fact, in contrast to the terse description of the first few months of the voyage, his narrative becomes almost verbose. Perhaps he had recovered from that brutal first leg, allowing him to take a keener interest in the novelties that surrounded him and his companions.

The fleet spent five days taking in provisions in the area. Gama named the river the Rio de Cobre after the natives' custom of adorning their

The river was called Rio do Cobre, after the natives' custom of adorning themselves with copper ornaments.

The Bay of Inhambane, Mozambique, was long-believed to have been one of the first landing sites. However, given the difficulties of navigating the bay, Gama probably landed to the south.

arms, legs and hair with copper. But Velho and his companions were so impressed with their reception that they called the area Terra da Boa Gente—land of the good people. Unfortunately, it was less than representative of the receptions that awaited them yet.

Once it left, the fleet stayed out to sea for several days to avoid the treacherous shoals and strong currents near the shore. In the process it passed Sofala, which Pêro de Covilhã had visited some ten years earlier, and the mouth of the Zambezi River. Without a local pilot or information, Gama had no way of knowing this. Instead he approached the coast near today's Quelimane. Many of his men were getting seriously affected by scurvy, "their feet and hands swelling, and their gums growing over their teeth so that they could not eat," as Velho sadly observed.

The ships, too, needed a break, so Gama ordered the necessary repairs. Velho seems to have remained in good health and spirits during the one-month stay and took time to update his diary. He described the natives as "black and well made," adding that they "took much delight in us." Fortunately they were also very friendly, delivering "in their dug-outs what they had, whilst we went into their village to procure water."

A few days later, Velho recounted, two merchants came to see them. "They were very haughty and valued nothing which we gave them." It was a sign of things to come, but the Portuguese took their rude behavior as a good token, since the merchants reportedly had often seen great ships manned by light-skinned men. As Velho pointed out, "this gladdened our hearts, for it appeared as if we were really approaching the bourne of our desires."

After seven months of traveling, "civilization" appeared to be drawing near. And so indeed it did.

On Thursday the 1st of March we sighted islands and the mainland, but as it was late we stood out to sea and lay to till morning.

We then approached the island and perceived some sailing boats approaching from a village in order to welcome the captain-major and his brother. As we continued in the direction of our proposed anchorage, these boats followed us all the while. When we had cast anchor in the roadstead, seven or eight of them approached, the people in them playing trumpets. They invited us to proceed further into the bay, offering to take us into port if we desired. Those among them who boarded our ships ate and drank what we did, and went their way when they were satisfied.

Because of the friendliness of the locals, the Portuguese called their first landing site Terra da Boa Gente—the land of the good people.

Gama and his men had anchored off the island of Mozambique——one of a string of independent city-states along the East African coast. But Velho was mistaken when he assumed the dhows that came out were there to welcome them. While the Mozambicans were cordial at first, they grew hostile after finding out they were dealing with Christians. There was no such mistake on the other side. The Portuguese immediately realized they were dealing with Arabs, both black—local Swahilis—and white—traders from the north, whom Velho described as being "of a reddish complexion and well made." They wore "fine lined or cotton stuffs, with variously colored stripes, and of rich and elaborate workmanship."

There were four dhows in the port at the time, which Velho observed to be "of good size and decked." "There are no nails," he continued, "and the planks are held together by cords," referring to the Arab practice of holding hull planks in place using fiber cords. Before long the sailors were checking out one another's equipment. According to Velho, the Arabs had Genoese needles, now better known as compasses, as well as quadrants and navigating charts.

Gama would have loved to get his hands on one of those charts, but this was impossible. Once the local sultan knew his unexpected visitors were Christian, he refused to cooperate. Earlier promises to provide pilots were not fulfilled. Even so, the Portuguese gained much valuable information. Aboard Gama's ship was a former prisoner who spoke Arabic fluently. He was told that the coast farther north had many shoals extending far out to sea. There also were many major cities along the coast, he gathered, several of them with "Christian" populations.

The nearest "Christians" would have been lived much further north, in the Abyssinian empire of

A local ferry heads from the mainland for Mozambique island.

On March 1, 1498, Gama anchored off the island of Mozambique, one of string of Muslim city-states along the East African coast.

Mozambique Island became the most important port of call on the India run. The Portuguese developed into a splendid city.

Prester John, but the Portuguese were under the mistaken impression that most Indians were Christian. The notion of cities and islands with large Christian populations further north, therefore, wouldn't have struck them as inconceivable. When local sailors added that the imagined kingdom of Prester John was not far from Mozambique, and that it had many cities and a valuable trade, it was no surprise that the Portuguese were encouraged. It "rendered us so happy that we cried with joy," Velho wrote, "and prayed to God to grant us health, so that we might behold what we so much desired."

In spite of this and reports that "further on, where we were going, precious stones, pearls, and spices were so plentiful that there was no need to purchase them as they could be collected in baskets," the situation in Mozambique soon became unbearable. Vasco da Gama tried to placate the local sultan with some gifts, but once more it became clear that the Portuguese had brought the wrong set of goods. Corals, cloth, and beads had been suitable further south, but in Mozambique they made the wrong impression. Everything was treated "with contempt," as Velho put it, leaving Gama with few, if any, bargaining chips. On March 10, after a skirmish, he decided to move on. He "secured" a local pilot, and the fleet set sail.

Contrary winds prevented the fleet from making much progress. Two weeks later, Gama was still in the vicinity of Mozambique. Further skirmishes ensued when his men landed to obtain water, sowing the seeds of mutual distrust that would plague the relationship between Europeans and East Africans for a long time to

come. Nevertheless, the Portuguese would soon be back in force. Just a few years later they established themselves permanently in Mozambique and quickly developed it into the most important port of call on the India run. Ships would often spend weeks there, waiting for favorable winds. Thousands of sailors and passengers died in Mozambique as a result, succumbing to malaria and other tropical diseases. "There is hardly any place under our rule where more Portuguese lie buried," Barros would assert just fifty years later.

Leaving Mozambique island.

After spending nearly four weeks in the vicinity of Mozambique Island, the wind finally turned, allowing the three ships to set a course north.

On Thursday the 29th of March we left the island and as the wind was light, we only covered twenty-eight leagues up to the morning of Saturday, the 31st of the month.

On Sunday April 1, we came to some islands close to the mainland. The first of these we called Island of the Flogged One, because of the flogging inflicted upon our Moorish pilot, who had lied to the captain on Saturday night by stating that these islands were the mainland. Native craft take their course between these islands and the mainland, where the water is four fathoms deep, but we kept outside of them. These islands are numerous, and we were unable to distinguish one from the other. They are inhabited.

On Monday we sighted other islands, five leagues off the shore.

On Wednesday the 4th of April, we made sail to the northwest, and before noon we sighted an extensive country, and two islands close to it, surrounded with shoals. And when we were near enough for the pilots to recognize these islands, they told us that we had left three leagues behind us an island inhabited by Christians. We maneuvered all day in the hope of fetching this island, but in vain, for the wind was too strong for us. After this we thought it best to bear away for a city called Mombassa, reported to be four days ahead of us.

The island "inhabited by Christians" was Kilwa, whose king was among the most powerful along the coast. As Velho reported, Gama

Mombasa, Kenya. Gama's fleet arrived here on April 7th, 1498.

tried to reach it but the strong winds prevented him from heading back. It probably was fortunate, for Kilwa was a Moorish city. It is unlikely the Portuguese would have obtained the welcome their pilot led them to expect.

A few days later, just before dawn, the *São Raphael* ran aground, though she was several miles off the mainland. Her sailors warned their colleagues on the other vessels, who lay to nearby, waiting for the tide to rise. "There was much rejoicing," Velho recollected, when the ship floated off. The shoal itself was named after the ship, as were the lofty mountains, seen in the distance on the mainland. Two small dhows approached while the refloating operation was going on. One of them was loaded with oranges, which the crews happily consumed. "Better than those of Portugal," was Velho's verdict. A few of the merchants were invited to stay aboard, presumably to help guide the ship toward Mombassa.

Staying farther out to sea, the fleet sailed past Zanzibar and Pemba, both of them important trading centers. The following day the ships approached the coast. According to their pilots, they were now very near Mombassa, one of the most important city-states along the East African coast.

> On Saturday April 7 we cast anchor off Mombassa, but did not enter the port. No sooner had we been perceived than a dhow manned by Moors came out to us. In front of the city there lay numerous vessels all dressed in flags. And we, anxious not to be

outdone, also dressed our ships, and we actually surpassed their show, for we wanted in nothing but men, even the few whom we had being very ill. We anchored here with much pleasure, for we confidently hoped that on the following day we might go on land and hear mass jointly with the Christians reported to live there in a quarter separate from the Moors.

The pilots who had come with us told us there resided both Moors and Christians in this city; that these latter lived apart under their own lords, and that on our arrival they would receive us with much honor and take us to their houses. But they said this for a purpose of their own, for it was not true.

As Velho implied, it didn't take long for the Portuguese to suspect a ruse. For one thing, there was the reception, with just about every vessel in port dressed up—something didn't quite fit here. Late that night, a dhow came alongside the *São Gabriel*. Its crew obviously wanted to board, but Gama only let their leaders—"four or five of the most distinguished men among them," as Velho put it—aboard. They stayed for a few hours, but the Portuguese guard was up. "It seemed to us that they paid us this visit merely to find out whether they might not capture one or the other of our vessels," Velho later wrote.

The next day was Palm Sunday, and the sultan of Mombasa sent Gama a number of gifts, along with a guarantee of safety. To confirm these attentions, Gama sent two men ashore. They were shown around the city and returned with samples of cloves, pepper and other spices—exactly the kind of goods Gama needed. These would be loaded aboard the ships, the sultan assured, if only the fleet agreed to enter the port.

This was a tough decision. Many of the crew were not well, ill-prepared to face the long and uncertain voyage that still lay ahead. Gama realized that if he could load spices here, he could avoid the coming dangers and return, virtually guaranteeing the financial success of the voyage. He suspected a ploy but decided to enter port anyway.

Accordingly the ships hauled anchor, but the flagship was stuck and didn't move. To avoid a collision the other two ships immediately dropped their anchors, at which point every Arab aboard, including the Mozambican pilots, jumped ship. Two didn't make it out in time, allowing Gama to question them, an interrogation made all the more effective "by

Although much of today's traffic has shifted to Mombasa's modern container port, Indian dhows still call regularly at Mombasa's Old Port.

Built by the Portuguese in the 1590s, Fort Jesus in Mombasa remains one of the most impressive fortifications along the East African coast.

dropping boiling oil upon their skin." The trap was then confirmed. Orders had been given by the sultan to capture the crews the moment the ships tied up to avenge the incidents at Mozambique.

"After the malice and treachery planned by these dogs had been discovered," Gama decided to go on, even though he no longer had any pilots. A few miles out at sea the lookouts spotted two smaller dhows, and the order was given to chase them, "for we wanted to secure a pilot who would guide us." One the of the ships was captured, and though everyone in it promptly jumped overboard, it didn't take the Portuguese long to fish them out of the water. A quick interrogation made clear the dhow belonged to an elderly merchant and his wife. Sixteen others were taken, along with whatever was aboard.

This time no one was harmed for Gama knew he couldn't continue in this climate of hostility without some allies. So the merchant and his wife, along with the crew, were treated well. In return, they informed him that the fleet was nearing Malindi, another major trading center, just sixty miles north of Mombassa.

The fleet dropped anchor off Malindi on Easter Sunday, 1498. This time there were no ceremonies. No dhows sailed out to greet the fleet. Instead it remained remarkably quiet. Velho imagined the people of

Gedi was once an important Swahili trading town. It was abandoned shortly after the Portuguese arrival in East Africa.

Malindi stayed put, "for they had already learned that we had captured a vessel and made her occupants prisoners."

According to the elderly merchant, there were four "Christian," or rather Indian, ships in port, any one of which would be able to provide a pilot for the remaining part of the voyage. This prospect appealed to Gama. By now he had grown very cautious, and he clearly preferred an Indian to a Moorish pilot. He agreed to release the merchant to the local sultan so than he could convey the request for supplies and a pilot.

The ruins of Jumba la Mtwana, one of several trading towns that were abandoned following the Portuguese arrival in East Africa.

On Monday morning the merchant was rowed ashore. The Portuguese waited, uncertain what would happen next. After dinner, he returned, escorted by some of the sultan's men. He told Gama that the sultan wanted "to enter into friendly relations" and would "willingly grant . . . all his country afforded, whether pilots or anything else." Gama had heard this before, of course, but he sent word he would enter the port the following day. At this point, he didn't have a great deal of choice. If there were Indian ships in port, he needed at least to talk to their crews.

Fortunately, this time Gama didn't have to be concerned. The sultan of Malindi was a bitter rival of his counterpart in Mombasa. He meant what he said, perhaps viewing the Portuguese arrival as a means to get the upper hand in the rivalry. Accordingly, Gama and his companions were treated well, and a week was spent exchanging pleasantries and courtesies. To reciprocate, Gama released all the Moorish prisoners, a gesture that bought him a great deal of good will.

The sultan of Malindi and Gama met on a few occasions although Gama, still weary from his encounters in Mozambique and Malindi, refused to go ashore, diplomatically explaining he wasn't allowed to do so by "his master." None of the crew seem to have been allowed to go ashore either, though the monotony was broken up somewhat by several visits from Indian sailors. It gave Velho a chance to observe them up close. They are "tawny men," he wrote, "wear but little clothing and have long beards and long hair, which they braid." When offered food, "they told us they ate no beef."

Several of them knelt in front of an altar piece aboard the *São Raphael*, confirming the Portuguese assumption that they were Christian. Among themselves the Indians naturally conversed in their own language, but some communication was possible because they spoke a smattering of Arabic. From that the Portuguese got a warning.

Don't go ashore and don't trust the locals' kind words, they said, for "they neither came from their hearts nor from their good will."

Despite the warnings, the sultan of Malindi was cooperative and trustworthy. When Gama, eager to press on, became impatient, he was provided with a "Christian" pilot. Velho referred to him simply as "the pilot," adding that the Portuguese were "much pleased" with him. According to Barros, his name was Malema Canaqua—a distortion of his Arab title of master astronomer. Some historians have suggested it was Ahmed Ibn Majid, a Gujarati who was known to be one of the most accomplished navigators in the Indies, if not the world. It is doubtful, but if it were the case it would have been a great stroke of luck for Gama and his companions.

As Velho made clear, there was no question that the pilot assigned was a competent navigator.

Gama set out across the Indian Ocean from Malindi. To mark the occasion, his men erected a pillar.

We left Malindi on Tuesday the 24th of the month for a city called Qualecut, with the pilot whom the king had given us. The coast there runs north and south, and the land encloses a huge bay with a strait. In this bay, we were told, were to be found many large cities of Christians and Moors, including one called Quambay, as also six hundred known islands, and within it the Red Sea and the "house" of Mecca.

On the following Sunday we once more saw the North Star, which we had not seen for a long time.

On Friday the 18th of May, after having seen no land for twenty-three days, we sighted lofty mountains, and having sailed all this time before the wind we could not have made less than six hundred leagues.

The land, when first sighted, was at a distance of eight leagues, and our lead reached bottom at forty-five fathoms. That same night we took a course to the S.S.W., so as to get away from the coast.

On the following day we again approached the land but,

owing to the heavy rain and a thunderstorm, which prevailed while we were sailing along the coast, our pilot was unable to identify the exact locality.

On Sunday we found ourselves close to some mountains, and when we were near enough for the pilot to recognize them he told us that they were above Calecut, and that this was the country we desired to go.

That same day the fleet anchored a few miles off Calicut. A few boats rowed out to query the crews, but it was too late in the afternoon to go ashore.

On Monday the same boats pulled alongside, and this time Gama sent João Nunes, one of the *degredados*, ashore for a brief reconnaissance. He was guided to some Tunisian merchants, who spoke Castilian. "May the Devil take thee," was their greeting. "What brought you here?" "We have come in search of Christians and spices," Nunes replied, neatly summarizing Portugal's dual motive.

Kappad beach near Calicut. According to tradition, Gama and his men made their first landing on Indian soil here.

One of the Moors accompanied Nunes back to the ship, exclaiming, "A lucky venture, a lucky venture! Plenty of rubies, plenty of emeralds! You owe great thanks to God for having brought you to a country holding such riches!" Velho expressed astonishment, "for we never expected to hear our language spoken so far away from Portugal."

For the next few days the fleet remained anchored off Calicut. Since the city's ruler—or zamorin—was away at the time, there wasn't a great deal that could be done. Gama sent two messengers to inform him that a delegation from the king of Portugal had arrived with the necessary letters. They returned the following day with a message of welcome and the indication the zamorin would return to Calicut at once to greet his visitors.

Velho and his companions whiled away the time, observing the city and its people, presumably from the vantage point of their ships. His first description conveyed the usual assumption that Calicut was "inhabited by Christians." He went on to describe them as "of a tawny complexion. Some of them have big beards and long hair, whilst others clip their hair short or shave the head, merely allowing a tuft to remain on the crown as a sign that they are Christians." He also wrote about the differences in clothing that signify the various castes, though the Portuguese were unaware of the system. As far as they were concerned, these people were dark Christians who just dressed a little differently.

During this first week the fleet was ordered to anchor several miles north of the city. Since the pilots felt unsure about the safety of their current anchorage, Gama complied, though he didn't move as close to the shore as the Indian pilot suggested. At the same time he was told that the zamorin was back in town. The first official contact could now proceed.

At first things seemed to go well, with an emissary from the zamorin inviting Gama to the palace. Velho was one of the thirteen men who went with him that Monday, May 28, 1498, providing us with a unique eye-witness perspective. Dressed in their best clothes and equipped with flags and trumpets, the Portuguese made their way to the shore, where they were awaited by the governor of Calicut, who was surrounded by many armed men. Velho and his companions were ill at ease. "The reception was friendly," he observed, "though at first appearances looked threatening, for they carried naked swords in their hands." There is no question that the small group could have been overwhelmed right there and then. Paulo da Gama and Nicolau Coelho remained aboard their own ships with orders to sail promptly in case that happened.

Fortunately, there was no reason for concern. A palanquin was provided for Gama, and the procession made its way to a river, which they crossed by boat. Thousand upon thousands lined the river banks to watch their passage, aware that something significant was happening. The road into Calicut too was crowded "with a countless multitude anxious to see us." "Even the women came out of their houses with children in their arms and followed us," Velho recollected.

By the time the Portuguese reached the city, the parade had grown into thousands. Prior to heading for the palace, they stopped briefly:

> When we arrived they took us to a large church, and this is what we saw.
>
> The body of the church is as large as a monastery, all built of hewn stone and covered with tiles. At the main entrance rises a pillar of bronze as high as a mast, on the top of which was perched a bird, apparently a cock. In addition to this, there was another pillar as high as a man, and very stout. In the center of the body

of the church rose a chapel, all built of hewn stone, with a bronze door, and stone steps leading up to it. Within this sanctuary stood a small image which they said represented Our Lady. Along the walls, by the main entrance, hung seven small bells.

Many saints were painted on the walls of the church, wearing crowns. They were painted variously, with teeth protruding an inch from the mouth, and four or five arms. In this church the captain major said his prayers, and we with him.

Perhaps some of the Portuguese were beginning to have some doubts about this form of "Christianity," and later chroniclers reported some puzzled muttering. But none of that was conveyed to their Indian hosts. The Portuguese knelt when appropriate and crossed themselves when the priests sprinkled them "with holy water." The Hindu habit of putting a fine mixture of dust, ashes, cow dung and rice water on the forehead, arms and chest was kindly deferred. Gama gave his to one of his companions, letting the priests know "he would put it on later."

The appropriate rituals out of the way, the group proceeded to the palace. By now the streets and alleys of Calicut were thronged with people eager to catch a glimpse of these strange men. Even the rooftops were filled, Velho wrote, and the group had to force its way through the crowds. Some people were injured in the process; at one point tempers flared and knives were drawn.

Things were getting out of hand, but eventually Gama and his men reached the palace and were let into a small court where the zamorin, or "king," as Velho called him, awaited them. Velho took in the scene with much interest. The king was "reclining upon a couch covered with a cloth of green velvet, above which was a good mattress, and upon this again a sheet of cotton stuff, very white and fine, more so than any linen." There also were very fine cushions and above the couch was a gilt canopy, exquisitely embroidered.

While the zamorin chewed betel nuts, Vasco da Gama "saluted in the manner of the country: by putting the hands together, then raising them towards Heaven, as is done by Christians when addressing God, and immediately afterwards opening them and shutting the fists quickly." Gama obviously knew what to do, according to Velho. "The king beckoned to the captain with his right hand to come nearer, but the captain did not approach him, for it is the custom of the country for no man to approach the king except only the servant who hands him the herbs, and when anyone addresses the king he holds his hand before the mouth, and remains at a distance."

Calicut had plenty of pepper and other spices, but the trade was in Muslim hands.

After the Portuguese were fed tropical fruits "which tasted very nice," Gama requested a private audience with the ruler. They retired to an adjoining room. Through his interpreter, Gama told the zamorin that he was the ambassador of the king of Portugal, "who was the Lord of many countries and the possessor of great wealth of every description, exceeding that of any king of these parts." He explained that the Portuguese king had ordered him to India, "as they knew there were Christian kings there like themselves." He was here to establish a Christian alliance, in other words, "not because they sought for gold or silver, for of this they had such an abundance that they needed not what was to be found in this country."

Gama's explanation struck the right chord. After having been assured that the king of Portugal "desired to be his friend and brother," the zamorin replied he would consider the captain to be his friend and brother as well and that he would send ambassadors with him to Portugal.

That was a success of sorts, although if Gama said what Velho wrote, he had bluffed his way through a good bit of his first chat with the zamorin. Establishing a Christian alliance with Indian rulers was indeed one of the expedition's objectives, but the ships were supposed to return with more than newfound Christians and polite greetings. They also were to return filled with valuable cargoes, especially spices. And of that, nothing had been mentioned yet.

After the meeting the Portuguese were given a lodging nearby, where some other crew members joined them. They had brought "the captain's bed" along with "numerous things which the captain had brought as presents for the king." Unfortunately they were entirely inappropriate, as Velho noticed:

> On Tuesday the captain got ready the following things to be sent to the king: twelve pieces of striped cloth, four scarlet hoods, six hats, four strings of coral, a case containing six wash-hand basins, a case of sugar, two casks of oil, and two of honey.
>
> And as it is the custom not to send anything to the king without the knowledge of his factors, the captain informed them of his intention. They came and when they saw the present they laughed at it, saying that it was not a thing to offer a king and that the poorest merchant from Mecca or any other part of India gave more, and that if he wanted to make a present it should be in gold as the king would not accept such things.
>
> When he captain heard this he grew sad and said that he had brought no gold and that he was no merchant, but an ambassador; that he gave of what he had, which was his own and not the king's, and that if the King of Portugal ordered him to return he would bring far richer presents.
>
> Upon this they declared that they would not forward his presents, nor consent to his forwarding them himself. When they had gone there came certain Moorish merchants, and they all depreciated the present which the captain wanted to send to the king.

This was not a good sign, and Vasco Gama must have privately cursed the people who had loaded his ships with these embarrassing things. If simple merchants looked down on his gifts, how would the king react? He found out soon enough. The next day he obtained a second audition, but this one proceeded quite differently. If you come from a very rich kingdom, the zamorin wanted to know, why didn't you bring anything? Desperately searching for a way out, Gama replied he hadn't because the objective of his trip was "to make discoveries." It didn't work. What did you want to discover, the zamorin asked: stones or men? And if he came to discover men, why hadn't he brought anything?

There was no suitable response, and the situation deteriorated. When Gama requested permission to land his merchandize, the king objected. That could only be done, he declared, if the ships were moored and the cargoes properly unloaded.

In the end, it didn't make a great deal of difference. A week later the

Portuguese merchandise was unloaded, but potential buyers quickly turned away, saying that it was worthless. Of course, most of these merchants were Muslim. As Velho observed, "they bore us no good-will," knowing fully well that any Portuguese represented a threat to their own lucrative trade. "When one of us landed they spat on the ground," he ruefully added.

A few weeks later, the Portuguese merchandise remained unsold. For Gama this was a problem. Without sales he didn't have money. And without money he couldn't buy the spices he wanted to acquire. Working out some form of credit was out of the question. The Muslim merchants of Calicut and its surroundings had banded together, spreading word that the Portuguese could not be trusted. Eventually they convinced the zamorin as well, explaining that a Portuguese presence could only bring harm. Ships from other regions would stop visiting, they warned, and since the Portuguese obviously had nothing to give, it would ruin Calicut. To make sure that this message of impending doom sank in, they "offered rich bribes," Velho wrote, making matters for the Portuguese even more difficult.

Unable to buy a large cargo of spices, Gama implemented another strategy. He ordered every one aboard to go into Calicut in small groups. Each ship was to send a man ashore, on whose return another would leave, creating not only a permanent presence but also a means to buy various goods in small quantities.

Velho and his companions thus got to go ashore on several occasions. They "were made welcome by the Christians along the road," he wrote, adding that the Indians "showed much pleasure when one of them entered a house, to eat or sleep, and they gave them freely of all they had." The Portuguese took along shirts, trinkets and "other articles which they desired to sell," but the trading wasn't very good. "A very fine shirt which in Portugal fetches three hundred reis was worth here only two fanões, which is equivalent to only thirty reis," Velho observed, frustrated at the exchange rate. But they went

A market in Calicut. Gama's men were relegated to visiting Calicut's markets in small groups, hoping to purchase modest quantities of spices.

ahead anyway. "Just as we sold shirts cheaply, we sold other things, in order to take some things away from this country, if only for samples." That way the Portuguese were able to buy "cloves, cinnamon, and precious stones," albeit in small quantities.

The Indians visited the ships in turn, to sell supplies or just look around, in small boats that pulled alongside. "Many of them were accompanied by their sons and little children, and the captain ordered that they should be fed," Velho noted, adding that "all this was done for the sake of establishing relations of peace and amity, and to induce them to speak well of us and not evil." Of course, before long word spread around that there was a free lunch to be had aboard, and the ships were overrun by Indians. "So great was the number of these visitors that sometimes it was night before we could get rid of them; and this was due to the dense population of the country and the scarcity of food."

By mid-August, Gama was ready to depart. He sent Diogo Dias to the zamorin to inform him of his intentions and make a final request to obtain a larger quantity of spices, but this didn't work out as planned. First Dias was kept waiting for several days before being allowed to see the ruler. Then he was told the fleet would have to pay a hefty departure fee, "as was the custom of the country and of those who came to it." When Dias and his companions wanted to return to the ships, they were prevented from doing so. One way or another they got word to the fleet that they were being held prisoner, a fact that "made us sad, not only because we saw some of our men in the hands of our enemies, but also because it interfered with our departure."

It took another two weeks to resolve the situation. Gama captured some hostages of his own, who were exchanged for the Portuguese captives. But since he didn't get back the merchandise that was still on land, he kept a few Indians aboard. Several of them would be taken back to Portugal and wouldn't see their country again for a very long time.

The Portuguese had now spent more than three months near Calicut. Velho's rendering of the stay is a story of rising and falling hopes, trust and treason, and a great deal of misunderstanding—a story that would repeat itself countless times in the dealings between East and West. When the fleet finally left India, Gama had no more than a handful of spices and a vague promise from the zamorin that future trade might be possible, provided the Portuguese bring something more than washbasins. But far more important than the spices they brought home was the information collected on India's commercial possibilities. Velho's account makes clear that the Portuguese kept their eyes and ears wide open:

> From the country of Calecut, or Alta India, come the spices which are consumed in the East and the West, in Portugal, as in all other countries of the world, as also precious stones of every description.

> The following spices are to be found in this city of Calecut: much ginger and pepper and cinnamon, although the last is not of so fine a quality as that brought from an island called Ceylon, which is eight days journey from Calecut. Calecut is the staple for all this cinnamon.

> Cloves are brought to this city from an island called Malacca. The Mecca vessels carry these spices from there to a city in Arabia called Jiddah, and from the said island to Jiddah is a voyage of fifty days sailing before the wind, for the vessels of this country cannot tack. At Jiddah they discharge their cargoes, paying custom duties to the Grand Sultan. The merchandise is then transshipped to smaller vessels, which carry it through the Red Sea to a place close to Santa Catarina of Mount Sinai, called Tuuz, where custom duties are paid once more. From that place the merchants carry the spices on the backs of camels to Cairo, a journey occupying ten days. At Cairo duties are paid again. On this road to Cairo they are frequently robbed by thieves, who live in that country, such as the Bedouins and others.

> At Cairo the spices are embarked on the river Nile, and descending that river for two days they reach a place called Rosetta, where duties have to be paid once more. There they are placed on camels, and are conveyed in one day to a city called Alexandria, which is a sea port. This city is visited by the galleys of Venice and Genoa, in search of these spices.

Velho's description showed not only that the Portuguese obtained useful information in India; it also made clear why spices were so expensive in Europe. Because of the number of duties and middlemen, cloves and other spices often cost a hundred times more in Europe than in their regions of origin. There clearly was a fortune to be made in this trade, explaining why Portugal would seek to control it at any cost.

But before that could happen, Gama had to get back to Lisbon with his information. "Greatly rejoicing over our good fortune in having made the great discovery that we made," the fleet left Calicut in late August. A course was set north along the coast, but progress was slow because of weak winds. It took more than a week to reach Cananor and another to arrive off the Netrani Islands. Then the breeze picked up, allowing the ships to arrive off the Anjediva Islands south of Goa in less than a week.

On several occasions vessels were sighted, some of them pirates, others apparently sent from Calicut in pursuit. But superior fire power enabled the Portuguese to avoid difficulties. Feeling relatively secure, they took the opportunity to careen the ships. Finally, on October 5, the fleet was ready to set out across the Indian ocean. But unbeknownst to Gama and his pilots, this was the wrong time of the year to do so. As a result the homeward journey almost turned into a disaster.

Owing to frequent calms and foul winds it took us three months less three days to cross the Arabian Sea, and all our people again suffered from their gums, which grew over their teeth so that they could not eat. Their legs also swelled, and other parts of the body, and these swellings spread until the sufferer died, without exhibiting symptoms of any other disease. Thirty of our men died in this manner—an equal number having died previously—and those able to navigate each ship were only seven or eight, and even these were not as well as they ought to have been.

I assure you if this state of affairs had continued for another fortnight, there would have been no men at all to navigate the ships. We had come to such a pass that all bonds of discipline had gone. Whilst suffering this affliction we addressed vows and petitions to the saints on behalf of our ships. The captains had held council and they agreed that, if a favorable wind enabled us, we would return to India.

But it pleased God in his mercy to send us a wind which, in the course of six days, carried us within sight of land, and at this we rejoiced as much as if the land we saw had been Portugal, for with the help of God we hoped to recover our health there, as we had done once before.

Despite many indications to the contrary, the Portuguese continued to believe the Indians were Christian.

It was January 2, 1499. The fleet had made landfall near Mogadishu, "a large town, with houses of several stories, and four towers around it." Latitude measurements would have been very difficult here, but Gama decided to press on toward Malindi, where he was more certain of a friendly reception. Accordingly, the ships headed on, reaching Malindi a few days later. As Gama had hoped, the sultan proved cooperative, sending much-needed oranges and other supplies to the ship. But for several of the sick crew, the help came too late, "for the climate affected them in such a way that many of them died here." Velho himself seems to have managed relatively well. "We remained five days at this place enjoying ourselves," he wrote, "reposing from the hardships endured during a passage in the course of which all of us had been face to face with death."

Somewhat recovered, the fleet set out once again on January 11, passing Mombasa. It soon became clear that there were no longer enough men to crew the three ships, so the *São Raphael* was burned near the sandbanks on which she had run aground nine months earlier. Once her crew and cargo had been redistributed, the two remaining ships continued, passing Zanzibar and anchoring off Mozambique Island on February 1. Four weeks later the Portuguese reached Mossel Bay, where "we caught many anchovies, seals and penguins, which we salted for our voyage."

Much as in the first part of the diary, Velho dismissed the trip through the South Atlantic return in a few paragraphs, stating that the two ships passed the Cape of Good Hope on March 20, then benefited from brisk stern winds. Near perfect for sailing, they carried them from the Cape to the vicinity of the Cape Verde Islands in less than four weeks. On April 25, the gradually falling soundings indicated they were in the vicinity of the mainland. Though they didn't sight it, "the pilots told us we were near the shoals of the Rio Grande," close to today's Bissau.

Velho's account ends abruptly at that point, raising questions about his fate. Some historians believe he must have died, but other sources indicate that he stayed in Guinea and lived there for several years. As there wasn't much of a Portuguese presence there at the time, this is doubtful, but what happened to him may never be known.

Fortunately his diary reached Lisbon, though we don't know aboard which ship. According to later sources the vessels were separated in a storm. Nicolau Coelho pressed on aboard the swifter *Bérrio* and reached the mouth of the Tagus River on July 10, 1499—almost two years to the day after leaving. Gama waited for some time to team up again, then set course for the island of Santiago in the Cape Verde archipelago. There he chartered a caravel, hoping to reach the Azores in time for his gravely ill brother to get treatment, while the *São Gabriel* continued on to Lisbon. He didn't make it. Paulo da Gama died a day after reaching the island of Terceira and was buried at a local monastery.

Shaken by the death of his brother, Gama didn't reach Lisbon until late August, shortly after the *São Gabriel*. A week later he was formally received by King Manuel, who gave him the equivalent of a ticker-tape parade through the city. Afterwards Gama was give the title of admiral of India, along with a generous annual income and other considerations. His crew, too, did well. Only 54 made it back out of a contingent of 150, but they were handsomely rewarded and could bask for a few days in the glory of being called the *herois do mar*—the heroes of the sea.

Manuel had good reason to be satisfied. Though Gama returned with only a handful of spices, the king knew that the voyage could be repeated by his sailors, giving Portugal the opportunity of controlling an enormously lucrative trade. He quickly moved to stake his claim to it. Upon Coelho's return to Lisbon, even before Gama made it back, he sent a letter to Ferdinand and Isabella of Spain, reporting that his explorers "did reach and discover India and other kingdoms and lordships bordering upon it" and "finding large cities, large edifices and rivers, and great populations, among whom is carried on all the trade in spices and precious stones." "We are aware that your Highnesses will hear of these things with much pleasure and satisfaction," he added.

Whether Ferdinand and Isabella acknowledged all of this with "much pleasure and satisfaction" is not quite so certain. After all, Vasco da Gama's voyage indicated that their explorer, who had set out to the Indies six years earlier, probably hadn't reached Asia at all. Columbus himself never wavered in his belief, but they had privately begun to doubt it. Up to that point the voyages west hadn't returned with more than a few natives, colorful feathers, and small amounts of gold dust. The "spices and precious stones" their Portuguese counterpart gloatingly described had yet to find their way back to Spain. But there wasn't a great deal the Spanish king and queen could do. The Treaty of Tordesillas, negotiated just four years earlier, gave Spain

The Portuguese would establish their first stronghold in India in Cochin.

everything west of the demarcation line and Portugal whatever lay to the east. It seemed that Portugal, not Spain, had hit the jackpot.

No one else in Europe was even remotely able to contest the Portuguese claim, so Manuel planned to consolidate his position. Of course he knew there would be obstacles. The voyage was long and dangerous, and very costly, both in funds and in lives. As Vasco da Gama had found out, it was clear that the Muslims along both coasts of the Indian Ocean were both numerous and unlikely to cooperate. Their resistance would have to be broken, which was bound to be difficult. In fact, others might have ruled it out, but Manuel was still convinced that the Indians were Christians. A two-pronged Christian alliance, he figured, should be sufficient to expel the Moors. "We hope, with the help of God, that the great trade which now enriches the Moors of those parts, through whose hands it passes without the intervention of other persons or peoples, shall, in consequence of our regulations be diverted to the natives and ships of our own kingdom," he wrote to his Spanish counterparts, "so that henceforth Christendom shall be able to provide itself with these spices and precious stones."

It was an ambitious, if not outrageous, plan. Here a small kingdom at the edge of Europe was proposing to divert the lucrative East-West trade to its own coffers, a plan bound to be opposed by virtually all of Islam. But that was exactly what Portugal set out to do next.

Within months of Gama's return, another expedition was ready to sail. This time a fleet of thirteen vessels with no less than twelve hundred sailors and soldiers would make the trip. It was placed under the command of Pedro Álvares Cabral, who was only thirty-two at the time but had excellent connections at the court.

The fleet left Belem on March 9, 1500—a date recommended by Gama and his pilots because it would allow the ships to use the tail end of the southwest monsoon across the Indian Ocean. Once in India, their crews wouldn't have to deal with the monsoon rains and winds the previous expedition had encountered during much of its stay.

Cabral followed Gama's course but sailed further out into the South Atlantic. On April 22, lookouts sighted land. A day later a boat was landed to scout it. A small group of people armed with bows and arrows awaited the party, but they quickly put down their arms. In fact, within minutes the two sides were exchanging gifts: hats and caps from the Portuguese in return for feathers and a shell necklace from the local Indians. The fleet spent more than a week there, with the crews and natives mingling on land and everybody reportedly having a terrific time. When it was time to head on, a supply ship was sent back to Lisbon with news of the discovery. Thinking they had landed on a large island, the Portuguese called it the Ilha da Vera Cruz—the Island of the True Cross. It would later become known as Brazil.

The remainder of the fleet pressed on. It was an imposing sight: twelve ships heading for the Cape of Good Hope and the Indian Ocean. Unfortunately they didn't all get there. Cabral lost four ships in a terrible storm near the cape, among them one commanded by Bartolomeu Dias. The survivors sailed on, reaching Calicut six months after leaving Lisbon.

Cabral had brought along more impressive presents, including silverware and tapestries, but the zamorin remained aloof. His Muslim advisors kept warning him of the dangers of the Portuguese, painting somber pictures of a ruined economy and impoverished state. Of course they were concerned. Vasco da Gama had been gone hardly two years, and here already was a new fleet, far more powerful than the

Many churches, like the ones pictured above and opposite, still remind us of the former Portugese presence.

first. Unless dealt with, it clearly represented a threat to Muslim trade patterns.

The Portuguese meanwhile had drawn lessons from their previous encounter. Diplomacy was still important, but they no longer were willing to be treated like dirt. Cabral knew he had the fire and manpower to be more assertive and began to make subtle threats. He also demonstrated his willingness to enforce them. When a heavily manned rival dhow entered the port, he sent one of his ships to take it. According to a member of Cabral's entourage, the zamorin "marveled greatly that so small a caravel . . . could take so large a ship."

These tactics paid off, and the zamorin eventually agreed to allow the Portuguese to set up a trading post. Seventy men were left ashore to collect the first cargoes of spices, but trouble arose almost immediately. Calicut's Muslims rioted and stormed the depot, killing fifty Portuguese. Cabral's reaction was swift: he seized ten Muslim ships, slaughtered their crews and bombarded Calicut, killing hundreds more. With the city in flames, his ships hauled anchor and headed south towards Cochin.

News of the carnage at Calicut preceded his arrival in Cochin, allowing Cabral to get down to business quickly. The ruler of Cochin was a bitter foe of the zamorin, so he was inclined to cooperate. In a matter of weeks another agreement had been worked out, allowing the Portuguese to purchase spices and set up a depot where men could be left to acquire and store goods for the next fleet. In the end Cochin probably proved a better choice than Calicut. It was a major spice trading port, competing for business with Calicut. More importantly, Cochin actually gave the Portuguese a welcome of sorts, thereby providing them with their first foothold in India.

The fleet returned to Lisbon in July 1501. Several ships and hundreds of men had been lost, but that was almost irrelevant. The remaining ships were filled with spices: thousands and thousands of pounds of them, according to a report that circulated in Venice. Sold in northern Europe, they made Portugal a fortune.

Another fleet had already been dispatched, and the next one left in early 1502, once more under the command of Vasco da Gama. Realizing that it wouldn't be allowed to enter the Indian Ocean trade peacefully, Portugal sent a veritable armada. Gama commanded ten ships, which were to go straight to India and return with spices. Another five were to destroy Muslim commerce in the region, and five more were ordered to station themselves off India's Malabar Coast to protect Portuguese interests.

Several anonymous accounts of the trip have survived, providing a chilling picture of Portugal's brash behavior. With sufficient firepower to back up any demands, Gama no longer needed to quietly slip out of port if things didn't go as intended. Instead he boldly sailed into the East African ports of Sofala, Mozambique and Kilwa and forced their rulers to allow Portuguese factories on their territories. Any opposition or hesitation was dealt with quickly and brutally.

Along the Indian coast the Portuguese behaved even more questionably, committing atrocities whenever they didn't get their way. Arab ships, which had been trading peacefully there for hundreds of years, became fair game. Shortly after arriving on the Indian coast in October 1502, Gama seized a crowded dhow. All of the adults on board were forced to turn over whatever they possessed, after which they were executed and burned. At the end "only seventeen small boys were left," one of the accounts noted. They were spared, to be converted on the spot.

In late October the fleet arrived off Calicut. Gama didn't like the zamorin's defiant attitude, so he captured a small dhow, hanged all thirty-two men on board in full view of the city, and had them cut up into pieces. Their bloody remains were dumped into a small boat, a letter was put on top, and the boat was sent to shore. To enforce his demands he ordered the fleet to bombard the city. "We saw houses and palm trees collapse," one diarist noted. Hundreds of people were killed. A few months later, after Calicut had still not given in, he repeated the exercise, executing all prisoners and burning their ships and belongings near the shore.

Word of these atrocities spread quickly along the Malabar Coast. It allowed Gama to conclude trading agreements with Cochin, Colon and Cananor without having to bother with cultural niceties. Before long, his ships were being loaded with spices at various ports along the coast. In late February 1503 the fleet reassembled and headed back for Portugal.

After a difficult homeward voyage, Gama's ships arrived in Lisbon between August and October 1503. With rich cargoes of spices, there was no question that the voyage was a financial success, but it was a great deal more than that. Gama had initiated Portugal's commercial policy in the region. Depots were established at strategic points along the East African and Indian coasts, enabling Portuguese factors to buy cargoes and supplies which, in turn, minimized the time ships would

The sun sets along Cochin's waterfront, silhouetting the city's Chinese nets. They were probably brought here by settlers from Macau.

have to spend in various ports. To protect them well, armed ships were stationed in the region. Any resistance to Portugal's ambitions was to be met ruthlessly.

This policy was reinforced by subsequent fleets. In 1503 Afonso de Albuquerque was sent out to Cochin to build a fortress. In 1505 a heavily armed armada under the command of Francisco de Almeida, the first viceroy of what had become known as the Estate of India, took the process one step further. Establishing additional garrisons and fortifications along the East African and Indian coasts, it enabled Portugal to apply uninterrupted pressure. All Arab shipping was fair game, and countless unsuspecting dhows were captured, looted and burned. Their crews were lucky if they escaped with their lives. "As long as you are mighty in the sea, India will be yours," Almeida wrote to King Manuel. He was right, at least in this initial phase. The well-armed ships with their superior gunnery began to disrupt Muslim trade patterns.

To increase Portugal's control over the East-West trade, Albuquerque was instructed to block the traditional Muslim trade routes to the West: the Persian Gulf and the Red Sea. In 1506 he captured the island of Socotra off the Arabian coast and ravaged the coast itself. A year later he took Hormuz, at the entrance of the Persian Gulf, and made a tributary of its sultan. This gave the Portuguese strategic control over the traffic flowing in and out of the gulf. Blocking the Red

Sea proved more difficult. Albuquerque's attempt to take the port of Aden at its entrance failed, leaving Muslim traders one remaining route to western markets.

In 1509, Albuquerque was appointed to succeed Almeida as viceroy. Though the succession was marred by disputes, Albuquerque moved quickly to cement Portugal's presence in the East. He realized that there was a need for additional bases to support the fleet and consolidate the Portuguese position. Goa, the most important of these, was seized in 1510. Its capture "worked more to the credit of Your Majesty than fifteen years worth of Armadas," he wrote to King Manuel, encapsulating his belief that a centralized command was vital to the future of the Estate of India. And Albuquerque had his eyes set on more than India. No sooner had Goa been secured than a fleet was dispatched to the spice port of Malacca. Shortly thereafter embassies were sent to Thailand, China, and other eastern countries to seek trade alliances. Few succeeded, but Portugal gradually increased its presence throughout Asia, along with its share of the trade between East and West.

Vasco da Gama, meanwhile, lived in semi-retirement in Portugal. For some reason his relationship with King Manuel had deteriorated. Not the easiest person himself, perhaps he was tired of getting the runaround. Few of the titles and considerations promised after his two India voyages had been granted. Gama kept mostly to himself, living in Evora, the city where he had spent some of his youth.

In late 1519 the relationship improved, with Gama obtaining the title of count of Vidigueira, which Manuel had long promised him. Five years later, King John III, Manuel's son and successor, continued the rehabilitation process by appointing Gama Viceroy of the Estate of India. A very prestigious appointment, it required that Gama make the long trip to India once more.

On April 9, 1524, Gama departed Lisbon for what would be his last voyage. His fleet of fourteen ships reached India five months later, and Gama took up his post. The Estate of India was disorganized: corruption, disease and continuing Muslim opposition had seen to that. Gama was expected to implement reforms to restore discipline and proceeded to do so ruthlessly. But he didn't complete the task. Shortly after his arrival in India he became ill. The disease, combined with his workload and the climate, rapidly weakened him. On Christmas Eve, 1524, less than four months into his tenure, Vasco da Gama died in Cochin. The Admiral and the Viceroy of India was in his mid-fifties.

Gama was buried in Cochin, but ten years later his body was repa-
triated and interred in Vidigueira. In 1898, the four- hundredth
anniversary of his first arrival in India, it was moved a final time, to the
magnificent monastery of Jeronimos near Lisbon.

It is a fitting resting place. For one thing, his grave is no more than
a few hundred yards from where he boarded the *São Gabriel* five hundred years ago. For another, the monastery housing it was built with
money that poured into Portugal following the discovery of the sea
route to the East. And finally, not far from Gama rests Manuel, the
king who sent him to India. He called himself "King, by the grace of
God, of Portugal and of the Algarves, both on this side of the sea and
beyond it in Africa, Lord of Guinea and of the Conquest, Navigation,
and Commerce of Ethiopia, Arabia, Persia, and India." It was later
shortened to "the Fortunate," for Manuel's achievements wouldn't
have been possible without the tireless efforts of his predecessor.

The king and his explorer thus rest near each other. It is appropriate, for these two men left behind a world that would never be the
same.

CHAPTER 4

A Liar's Tale

In Africa they have their settlements,
of Asia they rule more than any other,
and if there had been more of the World
They would have reached it.

Luís de Camões
The Lusiads, Canto VII

> Whenever I look back at all the hardship and misfortune I suffered throughout most of my life, I can't help thinking I have good reason to complain of my bad luck, which started about the time I was born and continued through the best years of my life. It seems that misfortune had singled me out above all others for no purpose but to hound me and abuse me, as though it was something to be proud of. As I grew up in my native land, my life was a constant struggle against poverty and misery, and not without its moments of terror when we barely escaped with our lives. If that were not enough, Fortune saw fit to carry me off to the Indies where, instead of my lot improving as I had hoped, the hardship and hazard only increased with the passing years.

These are the opening lines of the *Peregriniçāo* (Travels), an account of two decades of traveling throughout sixteenth-century Asia by Portuguese merchant-adventurer Fernão Mendes Pinto. It is a somewhat depressing opener, but it is followed by one of the great stories of exploration: a unique eyewitness account of what was happening at the edge of the then "known" world, in exotic places like Cathay, Cipangu and Pegu, among countless others.

Like other travel tales, Pinto's story was popular at first. Published some thirty years after his death, it was read widely in seventeenth-century Europe. But once the novelty of Pinto's observations wore off, the book's popularity declined. Before long it was mostly forgotten except in his native country. And even there, the book hardly got the reception it deserved, with Pinto being branded a liar because of his undeniable tendency to exaggerate. Not that he would have been surprised. Misfortune not only hounded him, it also hounded his literary legacy. It is unfortunate, for there is far more to Pinto's story than meets the eye.

Little is known of Pinto's early years aside from what he decided to include in the book. The first ten years were a period of "abject misery and poverty," as he called it, spent in Montemor-o-Velho, a village near the university town of Coimbra. When he was ten to twelve an uncle agreed to take him to Lisbon. They arrived in December 1521, a date young Pinto remembered because of the funeral of King Manuel. Shortly thereafter, he joined the service of a "lady of very high birth," where he spent about a year and a half. Over the next ten years Pinto worked for a number of powerful people but wasn't making any headway. The pay was bad and his name never came up when promotions were handed out. It thoroughly depressed him.

In late 1536 Pinto decided that he had had enough. He was now in his mid-twenties, and it was clear that he wasn't going to be successful in his homeland. So he decided to go to India, to the source of Portugal's riches. Others in his position had gone there and returned with a fortune. Even more had vanished without a trace, but their fate was quickly forgotten. It was the success stories that were remembered and circulated among the less fortunate. Just as young men a few hundred years later were prompted by the riches of the vast American continent to go west, Pinto headed east. It wasn't fortune that carried him off to the Indies, as he remarked ruefully many years later; it was his search for it that sent him there.

Finding a passage to India wasn't a problem. At least one major fleet left Lisbon for the East every year, and the Estate of India was desperately short of young and energetic Portuguese. But few realized what lay ahead. Even then the voyage was considered "without any doubt the greatest and most arduous of any that are known in the world," as one Italian Jesuit put it. He spoke from experience, having made the round trip during the 1570s.

The huge multi-decked *naus* that sailed east supposedly had room for hundreds of people and their belongings, and for hundreds of tons of cargo on the return journey. But reality was different. Life aboard mirrored society, with noblemen and high-ranking officials somewhat shielded from discomfort. For the others, the twelve thousand mile voyage promised six months of hideous food, appalling living conditions and filth. Diseases were common and spread rapidly; on long voyages they killed many of the India-bound passengers. Sometimes only half of them arrived alive. If that weren't enough, pirate attacks and storms also posed threats.

Even so, many people went woefully unprepared. "Each year four or five carracks leave Lisbon full of them," the Italian Jesuit wrote, "and many embark as if they were going no further than a league from Lisbon, taking with them only a shirt and two loaves in the hand, and carrying a cheese and a jar of marmalade, without any other kind of provision." Not surprisingly, for many it was a one-way trip to a watery grave.

Pinto must have been better provisioned, for an experience that could have given him plenty of reason to complain was dispatched in a few paragraphs:

> On 11 March 1537, I left Portugal with a squadron of five *naus*. There was no flagship in this fleet, which was commanded by the following captains: the *Rainha* by Dom Pedro da Silva, son of the admiral Count Vasco da Gama, who was commanding the same ship on which he had brought his father's remains back to Lisbon; the *São Roque*, by Dom Fernando de Lima; the *Santa Barbara*, by his cousin, Jorge de Lima; the *Flor de Mar*, by Lopo Vaz Vogado; and the *Galega*, by Martim de Freitas, a native of the island of Madeira.
>
> Proceeding on its course, the entire fleet, with God's help, made port safely at Mozambique. As soon as the fleet was provisioned and made ready to sail, Vicente Pegado, who was in command of the fortress there, presented the five captains with an order to the effect that all ships arriving from Portugal that year were to proceed directly to Diu.

Up to this point, Pinto's trip is in agreement with the historical record. Documents in Lisbon corroborate the composition of the fleet that sailed from Lisbon in 1537, confirming that it wasn't headed by a fleet admiral, which was unusual. Though Pinto doesn't say much about the itinerary, the fleet would have sailed first to Cape Verde, and from there directly into the South Atlantic and around the Cape of Good Hope. A provisioning stop in Mozambique by then had become routine, and the request to divert to Diu made sense, because the city, Portugal's newest acquisition in India, was about to face a Muslim siege.

After some negotiation, two of the ships were allowed to proceed directly to Goa. The others, with Pinto aboard, sailed for Diu, reaching the city in early September 1537. The arrival of seven hundred well-armed soldiers was a "joyful occasion" for the local garrison commander. He treated his visitors so well that nearly everyone, including Pinto, decided to stay. It was a smart move, for Diu sorely needed the reinforcements. A year later, the city was attacked by a large Turkish fleet. The Portuguese held on to it, but only after a heroic defense.

Pinto decided not to hang around that long. After a few weeks he became restless and joined a naval mission to the Red Sea to collect information on the Turkish fleet that was rumored to be heading for Diu. The mission had to deliver messages to Portuguese garrisons stationed in Ethiopia as well, but Pinto had only one goal: to "be rich, which is all that I cared about at the time." He wasn't the only one. Most of his colleagues went along for the same reason, hoping that a few rich Muslim prizes would allow them to retire comfortably. But it didn't work out that way. After leaving the Ethiopian port of Massawa, the Portuguese blundered into a fierce confrontation with three Turkish galleys. Outmanned and outmaneuvered, they didn't have a chance. The few survivors, Pinto among them, were taken to Mocha, to be put on the auction block.

A few days later Pinto was sold into slavery, ending up with a cruel Greek Muslim "whom I shall curse as long as I live," as he later put it. The Greek "used me so badly during the three months I was his slave, there were at least six or seven times when I nearly took my life with poison." Realizing that he was about to lose his investment, the Greek sold Pinto to a Jewish merchant on his way to the great trading center of Hormuz. There Pinto's fortunes changed. Hormuz was under Portuguese control at the time, and ransom for his release was quickly collected. In a matter of days he was "free of the suffering I described" and allowed to board a ship heading for Goa.

But nothing ever went easily for Pinto. The ship eventually made it safely to India, but the trip along the Indian coast was delayed by more battles, so that the young traveler did not arrive in Goa until the fall of 1538—about a year after he probably would have expected to get there.

At the time of his arrival, Goa had begun to take on the look of Albuquerque's vision of a capital of the East, with broad avenues and stately buildings. It already possessed several palaces and churches, a major shipyard, and a well-equipped hospital. Living in and around the

The capital of the Portuguese Estate of India, Goa rivaled the largest European cities in size and splendor. Given its many churches, it became known as the Rome of the East.

city were thousands of people: Indian, Portuguese, and *casados*—the offspring of marriages between the two. Albuquerque had promoted intermarriage, reasoning the city needed a stable and loyal population to survive. The strategy worked. On more than one occasion the *casados* proved essential to Goa's defense.

Despite this strong Portuguese presence, Pinto didn't feel at home. He recovered from the wounds sustained in his various adventures but soon found himself on the street again, with few prospects. Even though he had reached his destination, it was clear he wasn't going to make his fortune there, either. Success, it seemed, demanded a trip even further east.

Twenty-three days after we arrived in Goa, finding myself destitute, with no means of support, I took the advice of a priest who was a good friend of mine and went to offer my services to a respected nobleman by the name of Pero de Faria. He had just been appointed captain of Malacca, and at that time he was providing free board to any and all comers willing to take advantage of it. He accepted me into his service and promised to look after my personal interests insofar as possible during his forthcoming term of office.

The ruins of St. Augustine, Goa. Once one of Goa's richest churches, its roof collapsed in 1842. The site is currently being excavated by India's Archeological Survey.

Unfortunately, there were further delays. Faria and his men were first ordered north, toward threatened Diu. The Portuguese had assembled a massive fleet in Goa to help the besieged city, but only as a bluff; they didn't intend to send it there. The ruse worked. Its presence nearby, along with the rumors and speculations flowing north, caused the Turkish forces to lift the siege. Pinto and his companions cursed their bad luck, asserting they "had all been so eager to meet up with these enemies of our holy faith," but privately they were probably happy to stay out of harm's way.

Faria's men were asked to help instead with the reconstruction of Diu's fortress, causing Pinto to say that "the fact that it had been able to hold out seemed more like the working of a miracle than anything wrought by men." There was a lot of work, in other words, to occupy the newly arrived. Even so, Faria was eager to get to Malacca to claim his new post. In the spring of 1539 he finally was allowed to move on. He first returned to Goa, which he left in April with a fleet of thirteen ships and six hundred men, Pinto among them. Two months later, they arrived safely at their destination.

Malacca was the main spice trading port of the East Indies and one of the most important cities in all of Asia. At the time, it was a relatively young city, which had only begun to grow into its own during the early fifteenth century. Since then it had expanded rapidly. Traders realized that Malacca occupied a near-perfect location as a transshipment port for spices from the Moluccas. It was located along one of the narrowest spots on the Straits of Malacca, making for easy access to Sumatra, and its harbor was mangrove-free and thus safe for navigation. In addition, the opposing monsoons met near Malacca, allowing for traffic to flow easily in and out of the Straits.

The city's rulers exploited these advantages, using incentives and low taxes to attract traders. Before long the harbor was thronged with ships from all corners of the East: Tamils, Malabarese and Bengalis from India; Chinese, Thais, Khmers and Burmese from the north;

Javanese, Sundanese and Sulus from the surrounding islands; as well as Persians and Arabs. They came to load cloves and spices and brought along their own products to be traded along Malacca's bustling waterfront. By the middle of the century, Malacca had grown into a booming trade center, allowing it to extend its influence. In the process it became a major political power, controlling the southern Malay peninsula, much of the eastern coast of Sumatra, and the islands in between.

It didn't take long for the Portuguese to grasp Malacca's strategic importance. By 1504 they had collected information about the city, most of it from Muslim traders in India. A year later, King Manuel urged his viceroy to send a fleet to Malacca to establish trade and diplomatic relations. When that proved too ambitious, he sent observers, followed, in 1509, by a fleet. It was headed by Diogo Lopes de Sequeira, who was instructed to establish peaceful trading relations. As had been the case earlier in India, however, Muslim opposition prevented a successful mission. Several Portuguese were killed or captured, and the remainder barely made their way back to Goa.

Afonso de Albuquerque swore vengeance. In 1511 he sent out a new fleet, this time with an ultimatum. If Malacca didn't agree to a trade agreement, it would be taken. The Portuguese came equipped for the task and, after a violent battle, the city fell. Realizing that the ousted defenders would try to retake it, Albuquerque immediately ordered the construction of a fortress. Everyone was put to work—slaves, captives, even inhabitants. Mosques were razed and their stones used to build

Malacca's waterfront. Though quiet now, this was once one of the busiest ports in all of Asia.

Malacca's A Famosa gate is possibly all that remains of the fortifications the Portuguese had constructed here.

the walls. Standing high above the city, it served as an impressive reminder that the Portuguese intended to develop Malacca into a stronghold.

With Hormuz, Goa, and Malacca, Portugal possessed a powerful axis of Eastern trading ports, but even that was not sufficient. Just a year later, ships were dispatched from Malacca to the Moluccas, the fabled Spice Islands. They reached the Banda Islands and clove-scented Ternate a year later. In subsequent years the Portuguese sailed even farther. By 1515 they had reached the island of Timor, attracted by reports of its abundant stands of precious sandalwood. From Timor it is only a few hundred miles to Australia. The Portuguese would have been told of the land further south, and it is possible that Cristóvão de Mendonça or Gomes Sequeira reached it during the 1520s. But if they had, they would have quickly determined that there wasn't much to be traded there, explaining the absence of records.

When Pinto arrived in Malacca in 1539, ships were regularly shuttling back and forth with spices from Portuguese trading stations in the Moluccas. There the spices were transferred to other vessels for the trip to Goa and Portugal. Although Malacca hadn't recaptured the vitality it had possessed before the Portuguese takeover, it remained the main trading center of the region. The new rulers had made sure to put the various merchant communities at ease. The port, as a result, remained busy. Chinese, Indian, and, especially, local vessels used the northeast monsoon to move up the Straits, and after unloading and loading their cargoes, used the southwest monsoon to return home. Whoever controlled Malacca had "Venice by the throat," as one Portuguese observer put it, which was reason enough for Portugal to hold on to it.

But doing so was difficult. With no more than a few hundred men in the region at any one time, the Portuguese were far too thinly spread to maintain a firm hold. By seeking alliances with local rulers they created a measure of security in their Far Eastern base, but the danger always remained. The deposed sultan of Malacca, for instance, had set himself up in nearby Johore and had sworn to expel the invaders. Like others, he had assumed the Portuguese, following local custom, would leave the city after they had thoroughly plundered it. But these invaders obviously had no intention of leaving, thereby creating much resentment. An even greater threat was posed by the Achinese of Sumatra, who quickly expelled the Portuguese from their island and constantly harassed them in Malacca. The most powerful Malay state in the region, they were devout Muslims and thus equally committed to the ousting of any Christians.

Pinto received a quick education in the political situation of the region when Faria sent him on a number of diplomatic missions to Portugal's allies on Sumatra. It was a sobering experience. Not only did he have to suffer through a sequence of misfortunes, including a terrifying shipwreck, various battles and a miserable period of captivity, Pinto also began to realize that the Portuguese were in serious trouble. Although their ability to take advantage of Asian divisions had bought them time, it was clear that their allies no longer trusted them—with good reason. Promises were seldom kept, commitments were reneged on. On one memorable occasion, Pinto witnessed how a trusted ally and "good friend of ours" was defeated by the Achinese. The subsequent massacre of his people could have been prevented, Pinto believed, "with very little cost and effort on our part if, at the beginning of this war, we had given him the help he sought." Incidents like this began to make clear, to friend and foe alike, that Portugal was neither as strong nor as reliable as it appeared.

Who was to blame Pinto, diplomatically, left to the Almighty to determine, although he implied that the culprit was corruption—the desire by individuals, government officials as well as merchants, to enrich themselves at the expense of others, including their allies. Most Portuguese had come to Malacca to make a fortune as quickly as possible. Though Pinto was no different, it frightened him. He began to realize that their greedy attitude would cause the Portuguese to lose not only Malacca, but much of their empire.

Dutch gravestones at St. Paul's church as well as the Dutch architecture in the center of Malacca remind us of the city's Dutch period. Despite the odds, the Portuguese would hold onto Malacca for 130 years.

I have been so worried all along about our fortress in Malacca, whose importance to the State of India has apparently been forgotten by those who, by right, should remember it most; for the way I see it . . . we have no alternative but to destroy the Achinese or face up to the fact that because of them we will eventually lose the entire area to the south, which includes Malacca, Banda, the Moluccas, Sunda, Borneo, and Timor, to say nothing of the north, China, Japan, the Ryukyus, and many other countries and ports where the Portuguese, thanks to the intercourse and commerce they engage in, are assured of far better prospects for earning a living than in any or all of the other nations discovered beyond the Cape of Good Hope.

Moreover, if we should lose all that—which I pray that God in his infinite mercy will forbid, no matter how great our sins and the errors of our ways—we also run the risk of losing the Mandovi Customs House in the city of Goa, which is our most prized possession in India, since the main part of its revenue is derived from the ports and islands mentioned above, to say nothing of the spice shipments of clove, nutmeg, and mace that are sent to Portugal from those islands. I believe one can grasp the tremendous importance of all that is involved here, and once it is understood, I have no doubt that the proper steps will be taken to remedy the situation.

Unfortunately, the proper steps were seldom taken. If the Portuguese were able to hold on to their possessions, it was more often by default

Mosques dominate Malacca's rooftops, much the way they did prior to the Portuguese arrival.

rather than design. Pinto realized this, though it didn't make him lose sight of his own ambitions. His own chance at gaining riches came on one of his next missions, and he didn't ignore it. Teaming up with some of his countrymen in Patani on the eastern shore of the Malayan peninsula, he invested in a trade voyage to Siam, where huge profits were to be made, and set off with high hopes.

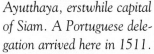

Ayutthaya, erstwhile capital of Siam. A Portuguese delegation arrived here in 1511.

By this time, the Portuguese were familiar faces in Siam. Back in 1511 Albuquerque had sent a delegation to the Thai capital of Ayutthaya, where it was welcomed. With hopes of finally establishing peaceful relations somewhere, Albuquerque next dispatched an ambassador, who succeeded in negotiating a trade agreement between the two countries. Compared with the hostility encountered almost everywhere else, this was a victory. For the first time Portugal didn't have to fight its way into a share of the eastern trade.

The agreement provided Portuguese merchants with access to Thai ports, so Pinto and his companions sailed for Lugor on the Gulf of Siam. Upon arrival their high expectations were confirmed. The cargo of silver they had brought would make them a fortune, they were told, and that didn't even include the possible returns on whatever they bought in Thailand. The prospect put Pinto and his shipmates in such a good mood that their attention slackened. It proved costly, for the same night they were boarded by Muslim pirates, who killed most of the crew, robbed them of their possessions, and unceremoniously scuttled the vessel. Pinto and a few of his companions managed to survive by jumping overboard.

Within an hour at most, Pinto found himself on the shore, penniless and devastated about his rapidly changing fortunes. Over the next few days his remaining companions dropped like flies, usually meeting ghastly ends, but Pinto survived—albeit barely. Near death, he and his last companion were saved by some local people, who nursed them back to health and even provided passage to Patani, from where they had set off with such high hopes a few weeks earlier. They also provided Pinto with some useful information: the pirates that had robbed them were led by a Muslim corsair named Khoja Hassim.

Back in Patani, the Portuguese investors in the enterprise swore revenge. Led by one António de Faria, they set off in a local vessel towards the coast of Indochina. Pinto went along, having no option "because I had not a farthing to my name." But there was more to the trip than mere revenge. Faria explained that they would explore "the ports and inlets along the coast," and pick up "some decent plunder to make up for the few shortages that still existed." No one on board objected; the Portuguese felt wronged, and robbing others to make up for what they had lost seemed perfectly justified.

Faria's strategy proved so lucrative that over the next few weeks Pinto and his companions became pirates themselves, attacking local shipping while supposedly pursuing their nemesis. In true Pinto fashion, a storm or other setback would cause them to lose everything, but whatever was lost was quickly restored with one rich prize after another falling their way. They even managed to catch up with Khoja Hassim, defeating him in a heated battle. Not a single one of his cohorts was left alive. Even the sick and wounded, who had been recovering on shore, were slaughtered to the last man.

As far the Portuguese were concerned, justice had been served. They had retrieved what they had lost and gained whatever else was in the holds of the pirate ships. Even so, none had a desire to return to a more honest occupation. Pinto and his companions felt that much of this was beyond their control anyway. If they defeated the pirates, it was because God had sent the enemies of the faith their way and granted them a glorious victory. If they robbed innocent victims, it was because the good Lord wanted them to enjoy the spoils. And if, in contrast, a storm or shipwreck made them lose everything, it was because the Almighty was punishing them for their many sins.

Historians now feel that Pinto's swashbuckling adventures in the South China Sea probably served as a parody of the overseas actions of Portugal itself. After all, the country was involved in unscrupulous dealings all over East Asia, from Timor in the south to Borneo and the Moluccas, and even Thailand and Burma. Like Pinto and his companions, Portugal justified its greed with religious excuses. And like them, it was constantly searching for new opportunities. One in particular proved a tempting target.

Pinto and his comrades in arms were operating near it at the time. His description makes it clear that this was a place with a lot to offer:

Both coasts were dotted with small settlements of some two

hundred to five hundred inhabitants, and though some of them were surrounded by brick walls, they were hardly strong enough to defend themselves against an attack by a company of some thirty decent soldiers, because the people there are all fainthearted.

But as for the location of the area itself, it is the best and the most fertile and bounteous in all things of any that I have ever seen; and there is so much cattle that it would be impossible to even hazard a guess at the number; and there are huge expanses of wide, flat, open fields of wheat, rice, barley, millet, and many different kinds of vegetables, the sight of which left us all gaping in amazement; and in some parts there were huge forests of chestnut, pine, and angely trees like the ones that grow in India, which could be used for building an infinite number of ships; and . . . the area is also rich in mines . . . to say nothing of the many fields of good fertile land lying fallow, and all of it wasted on those fainthearted people, for if it were in our possession, perhaps we would be far better off than we are these days in India, sinners that we are.

The Forbidden City, Beijing. Pinto often extolled the wonders of China, even though he got to see most of it from captivity.

While sailing along the Chinese coast or, occasionally, heading inland, Pinto often fell into similar exclamations of wonder about the riches of China. ". . . I say in all truth that I cannot find enough words that would do credit to it," he wrote, "for this land of China excels above all others in that it has a greater abundance of everything one could desire, more so than all other countries in the world."

These weren't merely observations from someone who looked at China only from a distance, for Pinto later got plenty of time to get to know the country intimately. At one

point in his travels he was shipwrecked and roamed along the coast with a few companions, living off the land and whatever people gave them. Of course, with Pinto's luck, this couldn't last. A few weeks later they were captured and taken to Nanking, where they were imprisoned and flogged so cruelly "that the whole ground was covered with our blood." They were then sent in chains to Peking to appeal their sentence. It wasn't a pleasant way to travel, yet Pinto never failed to sing China's praises. Nanking, at that time the country's second largest city, was described in superlatives: 800,000 people; 24,000 mandarin homes; 130 slaughterhouses, "with eighty butchering blocks in each"; and 8,000 streets, the most elegant of which had "heavy brass railings fashioned by lathe, running along both sides of the street." "I am already beginning to worry about how I will be able to describe even the little that we did see of it," he added.

A few weeks later Pinto and his surviving companions arrived in Peking, which he praised even more. "A metropolis that truly stands far above all other cities of the world," he said, "for its grandeur, good government, bounty, wealth, and everything else that one can possibly think of." "One should not imagine for a moment that it is anything like Rome, Constantinople, Venice, Paris, London, Seville, Lisbon, or any of the great cities of Europe, no matter how famous or populous," he continued, "for I dare say that all of them put together cannot compare with the least thing, let alone the sum total of all the grandiose and sumptuous things that make up this great city."

In spite of this flattering description, the verdict in Peking went against him, with Pinto and his remaining companions sentenced to hard labor on the Great Wall. Though this was hardly an enticing prospect, Pinto remained impressed. "In the twenty-one years that my misfortunes lasted," he wrote, "I can solemnly declare, in all truth, that not even all [countries] put together, let alone taken separately, can compare what China alone has to offer in these things."

This was lavish praise from one who wasn't treated well by the Chinese, but perhaps Pinto was again mirroring Portuguese attitudes. At that time, Portugal was bending over backwards to please the Chinese in an attempt to obtain trading privileges, but to no avail. Like Pinto, it was considered barbarian and constantly rebuffed.

Portugal had its sights set on the Middle Kingdom from the moment it first reached Asian waters. As early as 1513 Jorge Álvares had arrived in China, and for some time the two countries exchanged pleasantries. In 1516 Portugal followed up by appointing the chemist Tomé Pires as ambassador to the Chinese court. Shortly thereafter, however, difficulties began to emerge. Pires was a sensitive and intelligent man, which couldn't be said of all Portuguese. Not understanding why the Chinese refused to allow them to build fortresses, for instance, they conveyed their displeasure in high-handed tones to the local authorities. They also constantly reinforced their "barbarian" image by inappropriate behavior. Firing cannon shots when entering a port might have been considered polite in Portugal, but in China it was considered extremely rude. Flogging a Chinese official was an act bordering on stupidity. In short, Pires's mission was bound to fail, because his companions assumed they could deal with China on their terms, which wasn't the way the Middle Kingdom worked.

There also were other factors. The previous ruler of Malacca had been a Chinese tributary, which entitled him to Chinese help. The emperor hadn't responded to his pleas for assistance, but he wasn't going to welcome the Portuguese either. In fact, since they "were not as trustworthy and peace-loving" as he had been led to believe, he ordered them out of the country. Pires did everything he could to change the ruling, but in vain. Before long he himself was imprisoned and was never allowed to leave.

China's official attitude was a disappointment to Portuguese merchants, but it didn't keep them away. They knew that there was a fortune to be made, so they continued trading, albeit clandestinely.

St. Paul's was once Macau's grandest building, but a fire destroyed it, leaving only its facade.

Various places along the coast of Fukien and Chekian retained a Portuguese presence, where traders settled to buy whatever they knew would sell in Malacca—or anywhere else. Pinto met some of them in Chin-Hai, which he referred to as Ning-po. It appeared that they had made themselves comfortable in the area:

> Within six days we reached the Gates of Ning-po, which are actually two islands located three leagues from where the Portuguese traded in those days. It was a town they had built ashore with over a thousand houses that was governed by a city council, a high court magistrate, constables, six or seven judges, and administrative officers of state, where the notaries would sign the legal documents they drew up in the following manner: "I, So and so, Notary Public of the Archives and Judiciary of the city of Ning-po, in the name of His Majesty, the King. . . ," as though it were situated between Santarem and Lisbon. And they felt so sure of themselves and were so complacent about it that they had gone so far as to build homes costing between three and four thousand cruzados, all of which, from large to small, were later destroyed and completely leveled by the Chinese—for our sins—with not a trace of them left to show for it . . .

Historians doubt the extent of Pinto's claim, believing that the Portuguese presence was far more modest. But there is no doubt that Portuguese merchants operated from various sites along the Chinese coast and managed for several years to evade the imperial edicts. Sometimes their settlements were destroyed, but often they were left to themselves, especially if they paid bribes. And in one place they even managed to obtain formal permission. In 1554 some Portuguese merchants worked out an agreement with local Chinese authorities to settle in Macau, possibly in return for a commitment to cleanse the area of pirates. Three years later their presence was officially sanctioned. It finally gave the Portuguese their long-sought foothold in China.

Macau [Macao] was a small fishing village when the Portuguese first arrived, but they lost no time in turning it into a major trading center. To them, China was nothing less than a gold mine, and in Macau they were sitting on its doorstep. Not surprisingly, they made a fortune. Chinese porcelain and silk were very popular in Europe, and huge quantities of both were shipped home by way of Goa, particularly toward the end of the sixteenth century. Other Chinese crafts, from screens to religious figures sculpted in ivory, also made their way to Lisbon and the rest of Europe.

Macau gained even more from its role in inter-Asian trade. Portuguese merchants carried goods between China, India, Southeast Asia and everywhere in between, profiting handsomely from the mark-up in prices. And during the early 1540s, when Pinto was supposedly roaming the area, they made one of their most important discoveries yet. In fact, Pinto claimed it for himself.

Once he and his companions managed to get themselves out of their term of forced labor, they made their way to Sancian Island, where Portuguese merchants were known to be active. They hoped to find passage to Malacca there, but arrived too late in the season, all vessels having left a few days earlier. On they went to Lampacau, but no passage to Malacca was to be found there, either. To avoid the bleak prospect of a winter on the island, Pinto and two of his companions shipped out on a pirate junk, hoping to get anywhere at all.

Unfortunately, the ship was caught in a typhoon and driven far off course. Battered, it drifted for another twenty-three days before the crew finally sighted land.

> Coming closer to see if it showed any sign of an inlet or harbor with good anchorage, we noticed a huge fire burning over to the south, almost at a level with the horizon. This led us to believe it was probably inhabited and that there might be people here who would sell us water, which we were running short of.
>
> As we were anchoring opposite the island . . . two small canoes with six men on board came running out from shore. They came alongside, and after an exchange of greetings and courtesies in their fashion, they asked us whence the junk had come. Our answer was that we had come from China, bringing merchandise to trade with them, if they would give us leave to do so. One of them replied that as long as we paid the duties that were customarily charged in Japan, which was the name of that big landmass ahead of us, the nautoquim, lord of that island of Tanegashima, would readily grant us permission. He followed this up by telling us everything else that we needed to know and showed us the port where we were supposed to anchor.
>
> Filled with excitement we immediately hauled in our moorings and . . . moved in to drop anchor in a little bay to the south where a large town called Miyagima was located, from which many prows

Tanegashima, Japan. Along this stretch of beach three Portuguese came ashore in 1542 or 1543, becoming the first Europeans to visit the Land of the Rising Sun.

[prraus] came rowing with supplies of fresh food and water which we bought from them.

It wasn't a grand entry, but it is generally accepted that the three Portuguese who arrived on Tanegashima in 1542 or 1543 were the first Europeans to arrive in Japan. Whether Pinto was one of them is another matter. Few historians accept his claim, relying instead on the accounts of António Galvão and Diogo do Couto. As captain of the Moluccas during the 1540s, Galvão met one Diogo de Freitas who told him that the three men who had reached Japan were António da Mota, Francisco Zeimoto, and António Peixoto. Thirty-five years later Diogo do Couto, the official historian of Portuguese India, corroborated this account, adding that "a fearful storm of the kind the natives call *tufão*" drove them to Japan. Neither mentioned Pinto. He probably got the story either directly from his compatriots or through hearsay, and then wove it into his own account.

Even so, there is no doubt that Pinto visited Japan on several occasions, if not as the first European then clearly as one of the first. It gives his account a refreshing eye-witness perspective that is lacking in later chronologies. Besides, none of the official chronologies relate what happened right after the arrival of the junk. Pinto did, explaining that the local daimyo, or *nautoquim*, as he called him, made his way to the junk. Puzzled by the strange faces of the three Portuguese, he asked the Chinese pirate captain who they were.

Some sixty years later Nanpo Bushi, a Japanese Zen priest with access to relevant documents and original sources, set down the Japanese version of this first encounter. Called the *Teppo-ki*, or *Chronicle of the Gun*, it is in many ways similar to Pinto's rendition, although the islanders obviously looked at the event from a different perspective:

> At six in the afternoon on the twenty-fifth day of the eighth month of the eleventh year of Tenmom era, a great boat moored in the cove of Nishimura. We did not know from which country it had come. There were a hundred men aboard. Our people thought that they were strange because their looks were so different and because they spoke a different tongue.

Among the men, there was a Confucian scholar named Goho from the Great Ming. At that time there was in Nishimura village an official named Oribenojo who was literate in Chinese. He happened to meet Goho on the beach and with his cane wrote a question in the sand:

"The men on this ship are unusual-looking. What country are they from?"

Goho wrote in reply:

"They are Barbarians of the south. In general, they know justice and the rules governing relations between lords and subjects, but they are completely ignorant of the laws of etiquette. When they drink, they drink a lot, but they do not use cups. When they eat, they eat with their fingers and do not use chopsticks. They only follow their emotions, and they do not know the wisdom of self-control. And it is said that when barbarians reach a place, they immediately decide to stay there.

"Judging by what they brought, they are merchants. There is no reason to be suspicious. They are harmless."

The explanation apparently satisfied Oribenojo. Merchants weren't highly regarded in feudal Japan so the Japanese, while intrigued, weren't alarmed. Besides, Goho had assured them that these strange-looking men knew something of the relationship between "lords and subjects," which was comforting. But there was one thing these barbarians brought along that wasn't quite harmless. Pinto mentioned it almost offhandedly:

> Since we did not have any business to attend to, we passed the time away hunting, fishing, and visiting the very rich and majestic temples to their gods, where we were most cordially received by the bonzes, or priests, for the Japanese are by nature a very friendly and sociable people.
>
> It was during this time, when we had nothing to do, that one of the three men in our group, a fellow by the name of Diogo Zeimoto, who was very fond of shooting, would occasionally go off by himself with his musket, which he knew how to handle quite expertly. One day he came upon a swamp inhabited by an enormous number of birds . . . and while he was there he shot down about twenty-six wild ducks. The Japanese had never seen firearms like that before and they promptly reported it to the nautoquim. Astounded by the news, he immediately sent for Zeimoto,

who came straight from the swamp where he had been hunting. As he watched him coming towards him with the musket slung over his shoulder and his two Chinese helpers loaded down with game, he could hardly contain his excitement. From the way he carried on, it was apparent that he was simply delighted by it, for they had never before seen target shooting with firearms in Japan, and since none of them know the secret of the gunpowder and could not understand how it worked, they attributed it to some sort of witchcraft.

The *Teppo-ki*'s rendition is equally interesting:

> They carry a thing about two or three *shaku* long. This thing has a hollow interior and is smooth on the outside. It is heavy. The interior is generally open, but the end is sealed. At this end, on the side, there is a hole: it is through this hole that they put the fire. There is nothing quite like this thing.
>
> To use it, they put a mysterious powder into the hole and then add a small lead pellet. Then, taking this thing, he holds it against his body, closes an eye, sends fire through the hole, there is nothing he can't hit. When the shot goes off, it produces a light like a flash of lighting and a sound like a clap of thunder. Whoever is hit loses his soul. It is truly useful . . . .

The ruler of the island at the time was Tanegashima Tokitaka. Pinto reported, as did Nanpo Bushi sixty years later, that the daimyo quickly realized the importance of this "useful" thing. According to Pinto, Zeimoto presented his gun to the delighted daimyo and was handsomely rewarded for it. Pinto added Zeimoto then taught Tokitaka how to use it. Nanpo Bushi reported something similar, though with a uniquely Japanese twist:

> One day Tokitaka said to the barbarians through double interpreting: "I can't say that I know this thing well, and therefore I would like to learn about it."
>
> The barbarians answered, also through double interpreting: "If your lord wishes to learn, we will try our best to instruct you."
>
> Tokitaka asked: "Do you think I could master the secret?"
>
> The barbarians answered: "All it takes is having an honest heart and closing one eye."

Probably Zeimoto said something along the lines of needing to stand straight and squint through an eye. But something so simple for an object so magical gave the Japanese translator problems. So he interpreted "standing straight" as having "an honest heart." Closing an eye also led to some queries. Tokitaka wanted to know why one would have to close one eye, fearing that he would see less, but was entirely satisfied when his interpreter gave it a Confucian twist, "Lao-tsze said that to observe a little is to see better." At that the daimyo nodded, entirely satisfied that the musket's magic had been placed in the proper context.

Despite these charming differences in interpretation, it didn't take Tokitaka long to learn how to aim and shoot. According to the *Teppo-ki*, "Tokitaka polished the muskets in the morning, cleaned them in the evening and practiced with them continuously. In the beginning he was close to the target, but later he never missed it." The daimyo was also quick to realize the potential usefulness of the musket, so he asked his blacksmiths to copy it. "The shape came out quite similar to the original," the *Teppo-ki* continued, "but they could not figure out how to close the bottom." The Japanese blacksmiths overcame their difficulties when a Portuguese blacksmith, who arrived on Tanegashima a few months later, showed them how to use a separate piece of metal that could be screwed into the end of the barrel.

Within a year, Tanegashima's gunsmiths produced several firearms. Pinto didn't go into detail about the gun-copying procedure, though he asserted that "they lost no time going about it." By the time he left Tanegashima about half a year after arriving he said that "there were already more than six hundred of them around." On subsequent trips to Japan he never failed to be amazed at the spread of guns:

> All because of the single musket that the well-intentioned Zeimoto presented to the nautoquim as a token of friendship, to repay him in part for all the honors and favors bestowed on him . . . the land became so flooded with them that today there is not a village or hamlet, no matter how small, where they do not produce a hundred or more, and in the important cities and towns they speak of them in nothing less than the thousands.
>
> From this alone it is easy to understand what kind of people they are and how naturally they take to military exercise, which they enjoy more than any other nation that is known to date.

Japanese scribes reported more modest production, although there is no doubt that gun manufacture spread extremely quickly. Within months blacksmiths from Kyushu came to Tanegashima to learn how to make guns. Upon their return, they set up shop in places like Satsuma, Hirado, and Fucheo (today's Oita). Blacksmiths from the main island of Honshu went there to learn the process in turn, eventually setting up shop in the cities of Sakai, a major port just south of Osaka, and Kunitomo, north of Kyoto. There they developed the technology to mass-produce guns, ensuring their rapid spread throughout the country.

Naturally, it didn't take long for these guns to be used. The Portuguese arrived in Japan during the height of the "Country-at-War" period—a time during which independent daimyos were constantly at war, trying to subdue their neighbors. Although many samurai despised guns, feeling that they were unworthy weapons, others took to them remarkably quickly, and for good reason. For one thing, guns soon became far less expensive than samurai swords. For another, using them required comparatively little training, and it didn't require experienced samurai, either. Even peasants could learn to use them—a point not wasted on daimyos short of warriors.

Thus guns began to make their appearance on the battlefield. They were first used in a skirmish between opposing factions near Kagoshima in 1549. During the early 1550s, guns were also used at two battles near Miyazaki, although still on a relatively modest scale. But at the battle of Kawanakajima in 1555, twelve years after the gun's arrival in Japan, the air was black with gunsmoke. Just three years later, cannons began to be used.

Some daimyos continued to rely on their traditional samurai cavalry, but they could not compete. Nothing made that as clear as the crucial battle of Nagashino in 1575, where Oda Nobunaga defeated his adversaries, thereby consolidating his hold over much of Japan. Nobunaga took to the field with three thousand musketeers. They had been well-trained: after one-third had discharged their weapons, they stepped back to reload while the others aimed and fired, creating a constant barrage of fire which mowed down the opposing cavalry. After four waves had been massacred, the battle was over.

The battle of Nagashino made clear how much guns had revolutionized warfare in Japan. More importantly, it demonstrated how they had strengthened the forces that ultimately achieved the unification of Japan, and brought the long and bloody civil wars to an end.

Pinto didn't live to see this come about, although he clearly grasped

The beauty of Japan made a deep impression on the first European visitors, who described it in glowing terms.

that the introduction of firearms was bound to have a profound effect. On the other hand, he also realized the Portuguese owed their welcome in Japan in no small part to the guns they brought along, and it was a welcome change. In East Africa, India, and much of Southeast Asia they had met nothing but contempt, especially from Muslims. In China the reaction had been one of indifference or enmity. Wherever the Portuguese had gone in the East they had faced opposition, except in Thailand and now in Japan. Pinto thus spoke for many when he described his first visit in glowing terms. He certainly noticed life in Japan wasn't quite as idyllic as it appeared at first glance, but he wasn't there to criticize. After all, it didn't take him or his companions long to realize that there was a fortune to be made in trade with Japan, since no one else was servicing it. Here, in short, was the chance to become the exclusive middlemen in a very lucrative trade.

Accordingly, when they left Tanegashima, the three Portuguese made straight for Ning-po with a glowing account of riches for the taking. Pinto reported that Ning-po's Portuguese traders reacted immediately. They loaded a number of ships with Chinese silks and other goods and set off. He knew they were doing so at the wrong time of the year, "against the monsoon, against the tide, and against all reason," but he, too, was eager to cash in on his discovery.

Naturally, the venture didn't proceed as expected. The fleet was hit by a ferocious storm, wiping out nearly every ship. Pinto's vessel was one of those sunk but, along with a few others, he crawled ashore on Okinawa. Although condemned to death as pirates, the survivors managed to save their skins and return to Ning-po. With the Portuguese community there in an understandably sorrowful mood, Pinto didn't hang around. As soon as he was able to, he made his way to Malacca.

It is difficult to figure out just when Pinto might have arrived in Malacca, because his dates no longer add up. But it didn't matter. Pero de Faria was still captain of the city and promptly sent Pinto on a new mission. Over the next several years, Pinto traveled widely throughout Southeast Asia, from Burma through Thailand and south as far as Java, changing roles with regularity: first ambassador, then mercenary, trader, slave and prisoner. How much of this is true is almost irrelevant, for Pinto isn't talking so much about himself as about the Portuguese in Asia. Like him, they switched roles and allegiances at a moment's notice, provided there was money to be made. And like him, they constantly made sure that their dealings, however dubious, could be justified under the broad cloak of the "True Faith."

Money would bring Pinto back to Japan as well, although he had grown realistic about the chances of success. "I embarked to try my fortune once more in parts of China and Japan where I had so often lost my shirt," he wrote, "to see if this time I could better myself with another shirt less threadbare than the one I had on." At first it seemed he would fail once again. Upon arrival in Yamagawa aboard a carrack under the command of Jorge Álvares, the Portuguese found out that the prices of Chinese goods had collapsed as a result of the rapidly growing traffic between the two countries. Silk sold for a fourth the price it had cost in China, Pinto reported, "as a result of which we found ourselves faced with total ruin, without being able to decide what to do with ourselves."

But shortly after their arrival, a storm hit the southern coast of Kyushu, causing "every single one of these ships" to be smashed against the coast. Thousands of lives were lost along with all cargoes. Álvares's sturdy carrack survived, allowing the Portuguese "to sell their merchandise at any price they asked." It made them a fortune, though Pinto was distraught "that it had happened at the cost of so many lives and so much property, both of our own people as well as of foreigners."

Before returning to Malacca, the Portuguese took a Japanese fugitive aboard. Named Anjiro, he would play an important role in subsequent events. For in Japan, as elsewhere, the Portuguese wanted to import more than guns and trading goods. They also wanted to introduce their religion. Anjiro was just the man they needed to help them with this task.

As Pinto and other chroniclers relate the story, Anjiro met Francis Xavier, one of the founders of the Society of Jesus, upon arriving in Malacca. Xavier had himself arrived from Goa just a few days earlier, but quickly warmed to the stories coming from Japan. Álvares had left him a detailed description, not lacking in superlatives, and Anjiro came across as an intelligent man. From both he got the impression that Japan might prove a productive region for his missionary efforts.

A few years later he was ready to give it a try. Anjiro, by now converted to Christianity and fluent in Portuguese, joined Xavier and two Spanish Jesuits for the return to his native country. The small group arrived in Kagoshima on August 15, 1549, and was well received by the powerful daimyo of Satsuma. Xavier was given permission to preach and convert, and immediately set off to do exactly that. In the few weeks he spent there, he made several hundred conversions, which was quite a success considering that he didn't speak Japanese and had to rely on interpreters like Anjiro. But Xavier liked what he heard and saw. "The people we have met thus far," he wrote to the Society of Jesus in Goa, "are the best who have as yet been discovered, and it seems to me that we shall never find among other heathens another race to equal the Japanese. They are a people of very good manners, good in general and not malicious; they are men of honor to a marvel, and prize honor above all else in the world."

Xavier's glowing description was understandable. In comparison to the indifference, haughtiness, or hostility encountered throughout the rest of Asia, Japan was a miracle of civility. Wherever they went, Xavier and his companions received a cordial welcome, and people seemed generally receptive to his message. Even when they weren't, they were extremely polite about it. No wonder that Xavier called the Japanese "the delight of his heart." No wonder he began to harbor hopes that Japan might become the first Christian country in the Orient.

Quickly grasping the importance of birth and rank in Japan, Xavier focused his efforts on the nobility, hoping that their con-

A monument in Kagoshima serves as a reminder of St. Francis Xavier's arrival here in 1549.

version would cause their subjects to follow. Some daimyos in Kyushu converted readily, but Xavier had set his sights higher. He had already heard of the mysterious emperor who lived in Kyoto, and of the shogun—the country's military ruler. Though their power was very limited at the time, Xavier decided to head to Kyoto, hoping to convert them, or at least to get them interested in Christianity. He made the long trip to the capital with two companions, but in vain. The emperor was not to be seen, he was told, no matter how much he persisted. Dejected, he returned to Kyushu.

Xavier spent another year in western Japan. During this time Pinto arrived there for his third visit, a coincidence that enabled him to witness Xavier's reception by Otomo Sorin, king of Bungo and one of the most powerful daimyos in Kyushu:

> We all got ready as best as each one could at the time and departed for the city on board the nau's longboat and two manchuas covered with awnings and silken banners, with trumpets and flutes playing alternately from time to time. The local people were so amazed by this unusual sight that by the time we reached the pier, it was impossible to get ashore.
>
> From here, the Father proceeded directly to the palace on foot, accompanied by a crowd of noblemen and all thirty of the Portuguese with about an equal number of our slave boys, all very well dressed, with gold chains around the neck.
>
> The Father was wearing a cassock of black unwatered camlet with a surplice over it and a green velvet stale with a brocade border. Our captain was walking with a staff in his hand like a major-domo, and five of the most honorable and richest men of the highest reputation were carrying certain objects in their hands, as though they were servants of his. . . . In this order and with this ostentation, we passed through the nine principal streets of the city which were so thronged with people that even the rooftops, everywhere, were full.

This sort of presentation was very important for the prestige of the Jesuits. The Japanese already admired them for their discipline, but the fact that the Jesuits were obviously held in high regard by their countrymen, with powerful captains and wealthy merchants paying their respects, increased it even more. The fact that every daimyo with a harbor was eager to attract Portuguese trade also helped. When it was realized, for instance, that the Jesuits influenced which ports the ships visited, a good many daimyos readily converted. It wasn't necessarily a firm belief in heavenly so much as earthly riches that caused them to do so, but it enabled Christianity to spread much more quickly then it otherwise would have.

In 1551, Xavier left Japan. He died a few months later off the Chinese coast never having made it back to Japan, but he had laid the groundwork for the Jesuits' subsequent efforts and presence. Conversion attempts were to be concentrated at the top, cultivating the aristocracy and hoping that their subjects would follow. Trade could be used as an enticement. And every member of the Society of Jesus was to learn as much as possible about the Japanese, for Xavier realized that an understanding of their culture was essential to the mission.

In subsequent years the Jesuit presence grew, albeit slowly. Ten years after Xavier's death, there were only six missionaries in Japan; by 1570 no more than twenty. Yet their impact belied their numbers, especially in western Japan, where the Jesuits established a solid Christian foundation with hundreds of thousands of converts, among them powerful daimyos like Otomo Sorin. It enabled the Jesuits to obtain a base, not only for themselves but also for Portuguese merchants. Called Nagasaki ("Long Cape"), it was no more than a small fishing village in northwestern Kyushu at the time, but it had a superb deep-water harbor. Nagasaki wouldn't remain a village for long: once the Portuguese settled there it quickly grew into a busy port and one of the most important cities in Kyushu.

There were Christian communities on the other Japanese islands as well, although manpower shortages never allowed quite the same level of presence. Even so, the Jesuits traveled widely and circulated in high places. They also undertook a serious study of the country, sending back fascinating reports to their superiors in Rome and Goa. Far from looking down on what they saw, their observations were often appreciative, comparing Japanese practices favorably with their western equivalents.

Some of these reports covered day-to-day activities, such as eating and drinking and social behavior. Others provided a remarkably candid view of the Japanese themselves, offering insights that are relevant even today. And some observations took on a significance all their own, because they gave accounts of conversations with Japan's leaders. In 1569, for instance, Father Luís Frois met Oda Nobunaga, who was to become the most powerful man in Japan. "He would be about thirty-seven years old," Frois noted, describing the feared Nobunaga as "a tall man, lean, scantly bearded, with a clear voice, greatly addicted to military exercises, hardy, disposed to temper justice with mercy, proud, a great stickler for honor, very secretive in his plans, most expert in the wiles of warfare, little or not disposed to accept reproof or advice from his subordinates, but greatly feared and respected by everyone." No contemporary Japanese chronicler would ever have dared to provided such a frank assessment, making it invaluable.

Frois would meet with Nobunaga for the next ten years, chronicling his rise to the pinnacle of Japanese power. He reported on the destruction of the Buddhist sects that Nobunaga saw as his main threat, followed his subsequent battles, covered Nobunaga's views on trade and Christianity, and was nearby when the general was murdered in 1582. Frois gave one of the few accounts of the crime, asserting that the mortally wounded Nobunaga set fire to the castle and perished in the flames. "What we do know," he concluded, "is that of this man, who made everyone tremble not only at the sound of his voice but even at the mention of his name, there did not remain even a small hair which was not reduced to dust and ashes."

The Oura cathedral in Nagasaki is the oldest Catholic church in Japan. It was built after 250 years of religious persecution came to an end.

Other Jesuits made sure they got to know Nobunaga's successor, Toyotomi Hideyoshi. Father Gaspar Coelho, head of the order in Japan, was soon on friendly terms with the new ruler, but the relationship wasn't as cordial. Although Hideyoshi was as opposed as his predecessor to the Buddhist sects, he sensed Christianity could become a threat as well. His wariness was probably reinforced by the arrival of Spanish priests in Japan, following the unification of Spain and Portugal in 1580. Hideyoshi and his advisors noticed a difference. While the Portuguese usually focused on trading, the Spanish were conquerors and made no secret of it. Even their priests were more aggressive and less willing to put up with the intricacies of Japanese etiquette.

The reaction was swift. In 1587 Hideyoshi ordered all Christian missionaries out of the country. Most of them went into hiding instead, which seemed to satisfy Hideyoshi. He never enforced the expulsion order, though it served as a warning.

During the early 1590s Hideyoshi focused his attention on an invasion of Korea, a massive undertaking that provided Christianity a respite of sorts. Emboldened, the missionaries continued to sow the seeds of their downfall. Franciscan priests began to enter Japan from the Spanish-occupied Philippines. Unlike their Jesuit colleagues, who focused on the upper classes, the Franciscans believed in mass appeals to crowds of ordinary people, a technique far more intrusive and visible and thus more likely to attract opposition from the Japanese authorities.

This was asking for trouble. It came in 1596, when a Spanish galleon was wrecked off the island of Shikoku. The rich cargo was claimed by the Japanese, but the Spanish captain objected. He even made threats, asserting that unless the cargo were returned, Spain would conquer Japan. That sort of talk might have been dismissed in Europe without much thought, but in Japan it was very dangerous. Unaware, the captain persisted, adding that Spanish conquests were always preceded by missionaries to pave the way. To prove it, he had a few of them aboard, he insinuated. This proved to be a monumental blunder.

When Hideyoshi was told of the affair, he decided to set an example. Several Kyoto-based priests and accolytes were condemned to death. After a long and torturous march through the country they were crucified in Nagasaki. Twenty-six of them died: six Franciscans, seventeen Japanese friars, and three Jesuit lay-brothers. Japanese Christianity had been given another, more frightening warning.

The Twenty-Six Martyrs Memorial commemorates the twenty-six Japanese and European priests, acolytes, and lay brothers who were crucified in Nagasaki in early 1597.

Hideyoshi died a year later, providing a temporary respite. As long as Christianity was associated with the valuable trade passing through Nagasaki and the many benefits of European knowledge, it wasn't going to be eliminated altogether. In fact, Tokugawa Ieyasu, Hideyoshi's successor and the founder of the Tokugawa shogunate, was eager for European knowledge. Accordingly he was willing to tolerate the missionaries, providing that their activities could be controlled.

But in 1600 a Dutch ship arrived off Japan. Its occupants were just as willing to trade as the Portuguese and, as soon became clear, were willing to do so without any religious conditions. More importantly, they confirmed Japanese suspicions about the Spanish and Portuguese. Protestant Holland had gone through a long war with Catholic Spain, and the Dutch recounted the Spanish atrocities in graphic detail.

Perhaps they didn't come out and say so, but they clearly implied that Japan could well be next. Tokugawa made up his mind: the priests would have to go. The Dutch assured him that they would continue to trade, guaranteeing continued access to the benefits of European trade.

In 1613 all missionaries were once more ordered out of the country and Japanese Christians were forced to recant. This time the expulsion was enforced, albeit gradually. But the tide had clearly turned. Following Ieyasu's death in 1616, the attacks on Christianity were stepped up. Four clandestine missionaries were executed. Japanese Christians, too, faced execution unless they immediately recanted. The situation worsened when Ieyasu's grandson, Iemitsu, took over in 1623. He implemented a period of ruthless persecution. Thousands of Japanese Christians were condemned to brutal deaths. They died courageously and willingly, gaining the admiration of some and the hatred of others. In response, Iemitsu began the gradual closing of the country. He prohibited Japanese travels abroad and dramatically reduced the freedom of foreigners. Now all foreign influences were beginning to be perceived as a threat.

Nagasaki's O-Kunshi matsuri, one of Japan's principal festivals, commemorates the strong Portuguese influence in this part of Japan.

The process was concluded in 1638 when peasants in western Kyushu rebelled against the crippling taxes imposed on them. Among them were many Christians. What had started as a social rebellion was soon labeled a Christian uprising, confirming the shogunate's fears. A massive army was dispatched to the rebels' stronghold and after a long siege they were all slaughtered, nearly forty thousand in all. The Portuguese, suspected of having aided the revolt, were expelled. The Dutch, who had aided the shogunate by sending a ship to bombard the rebels, obtained an exemption—a few of them were allowed to stay, confined

to the small island of Deshima in Nagasaki harbor. All other westerners were forced out, effectively closing Japan to the outside world.

The Portuguese left behind a much changed country. When they had arrived a century earlier, Japan had been a divided country. Its ruling daimyos had recognized no centralized government. Trying to increase their holdings through force or treachery, they had created a period of near-constant warfare. The country the Portuguese were forced to leave, by contrast, was a stable one, with a highly centralized bureaucracy under the firm control of a shogun dynasty.

There is no question that the guns and bibles imported by the Portuguese played an important role in this transformation, but there was more. The Portuguese and, later, other Europeans brought a variety of goods into the country, including glass, mirrors, wines, spectacles and compasses. They readily shared their science and technology, instructing the Japanese in geography, engineering, printing and mining. They built schools, hospitals and shipyards. They introduced tobacco, and for some time it was fashionable in Japan to wear Western clothes. Most importantly, they brought a new way of looking at things. In line with their Buddhist beliefs, the Japanese had come to believe that much of life depended on fate, which in turn was influenced by the divination of the positive and the negative. Europeans, on the other hand, tried to explain things. The Japanese were hungry for this sort of knowledge. In one of his first reports to Rome, Francis Xavier asked for missionaries with a firm grasp of natural philosophy as well as theology. He knew that the Japanese wanted to know about these things, initiating a flow of information that sped up the country's transformation.

In the end, the situation proved unstable. The centralized government that the Portuguese helped bring about through their weapons and ideas soon felt threatened by the rapid changes. The new shogunate wanted to preserve its position at the apex of the power structure. Unsure of its ability to do so with a constant influx of new goods and new ideas, it evicted all foreigners and shielded the country from foreign influences. It managed to do so until Perry's arrival in 1853.

The high taxes imposed on local farmers to construct Shimabara Castle were at the root of the Shimabara rebellion.

The ouster from Japan was a major setback for the Portuguese. Control of the Japan–China trade had been very profitable and they desperately wanted to hold onto it. Their efforts were fruitless. A delegation sent from Macau to Nagasaki to plead the Portuguese case was promptly executed along with most of the Portuguese aboard. The door had been shut and would remain so for a long time to come.

By that time the Portuguese were facing increasing competition throughout the East, especially from the Dutch and the English. Their merchants didn't mix trade with religion, which was a considerable advantage in dealing with countries that had well-established religious beliefs of their own. Before long, the lucrative East–West trade began to change hands, and the Portuguese began to lose their bases. Bahrain was lost in 1602, the Moluccas were attacked by the Dutch in 1605, the fortress of Hormuz was lost in 1622, and El Mina was captured by the Dutch in 1637. Malacca, Portugal's main base in Southeast Asia, changed hands in 1641, not to the feared Achinese but to the Dutch, who teamed up with the Muslims to take the city.

And it was far from over. In 1652 the Portuguese base on Zanzibar was sacked. Mombassa fell in 1655, Colombo a year later. And so Mendes Pinto's fears began to materialize, long after his death but more or less along the lines he had predicted. Perhaps it didn't take a brilliant mind to foresee the demise. After all, Pinto observed time after time that he and his compatriots went East to fill their pockets. And he readily participated, in search of the elusive fortune that send him East.

Eventually Pinto did get rich, although he doesn't tell us when and where. It probably was towards the end of his adventures, perhaps on one his trips to Japan. He also doesn't tell us that he shared a good deal of his fortune with the Jesuit mission, apparently after having been thoroughly impressed with Francis Xavier. He even became a lay brother of the society and financed much of a Jesuit voyage to Japan, a trip he joined as ambassador for his fourth and final voyage to the Land of the Rising Sun.

But some time after that voyage, Pinto had a change of heart and left the Society of Jesus. He then made his way back to Portugal by way of Goa. He arrived in Lisbon in September 1558, twenty-one years after having set out, presumably with high hopes of being rewarded for his Asian service. But nothing ever came of that. Perhaps it was fortunate, for it was the gradual realization that the Portuguese court wasn't planning to compensate him that spurred Pinto into writing his book.

Small amulets mark the site at Hara Castle where the Shimabara rebels were slaughtered. More than forty thousand people perished.

When published in 1614, some thirty years after Pinto's death, the book quickly became popular. But it did so as a good adventure story, not for what it really was. Pinto's story is much more than a succession of shipwrecks, battles, and adventures as soldier, slave, pirate, diplomat, merchant and missionary. In many ways it is a parody of Portugal's exploits in Asia. Like Pinto, Portugal was trader, ambassador, missionary and soldier. And like Pinto, it couldn't do all these things at once. There was no way that a few thousand people could maintain a trading empire that stretched halfway across the globe.

The analogy extends further because Pinto's adventures mirror the Portuguese expansion to a remarkable extent. From the moment Pinto set sail from Lisbon, he sailed in the wake of his predecessors, first along the northwest African coast to Cape Verde, then along the route pioneered by Vasco da Gama. Once in India, there were his detours to the Red Sea and Persian Gulf—the two Muslim trade routes to the West which Portugal tried to close early in the sixteenth century. The Persian Gulf was secured with the capture of Hormuz, but the Red Sea remained open. Although they sent ships and fleets to the region, the Portuguese never controlled it, as Pinto's own capture there demonstrated.

The parallel continues with Pinto's journey to Malacca and from there into much of Southeast Asia, China and, finally, Japan, mirroring Portugal's expansion geographically as well as chronologically. Whether Pinto was actually present at many of the events he claimed to have witnessed is almost irrelevant. He knew the region well enough to work himself into its history, albeit to the dismay of subsequent historians. Many of his observations were new and refreshing, although they weren't published until sixty to seventy years after the events. And for those willing to read between the lines, they remain relevant today.

Finally, there is a parallel Pinto didn't include, though he possibly assumed its inevitability. In the end Portugal, like Pinto, lost most of its possessions. And, like him, it would scarcely be recognized for its pioneering role.

Perhaps that is to be expected. Motivated by God and greed, this story isn't always pretty. But the many Pintos that left Portugal and the rest of Europe during the fifteenth and sixteenth centuries brought back far more than spices and Eastern luxuries; they returned with a new view of the world, a planetary view that perceived different cultures not as isolated but as linked both physically and emotionally. It affected not only them, but also the people whom they encountered. And, having shaped the world we inherited, it continues to affect all of us to this day.

Evicted from Japan, the Portuguese were forced to leave, this time into the setting sun. But the country they left was quite different from the one they entered a hundred years earlier.

Biographies

AFONSO DE ALBUQUERQUE

Though not well known outside his native country, Afonso de Albuquerque is one of the towering figures of the Portuguese expansion. The second son of Gonçalo de Albuquerque, he was born in 1453 and raised at the Court of Afonso V. There are indications that he served at Arzila in the entourage of the king's son, the future John II, and in the expedition that led to a Christian victory against the Turks in Otranto in 1481. Little is known of his activities during the latter part of the century. In 1503, Albuquerque went to India for the first time, on the voyage which saw the establishment of a fortress in Cochin. Three years later he was sent to India once more, this time with secret orders appointing him Viceroy of India, succeeding Francisco de Almeida. Almeida refused to relinquish his post, however, and it wasn't until 1509 that Albuquerque was able to assume his command. He quickly implemented a far-ranging strategy, capturing Goa in 1510 and Malacca a year later, and sending embassies into China, Thailand, Pegu, and other Asian territories. Though his activities required Lisbon's approval, there is no question that Albuquerque single-handedly shaped Portugal's policy in the Orient, and thereby strongly influenced early relations between East and West.

GOMES EANES DE AZURARA

Gomes Eanes de Azurara was the official court historian of Afonso V, succeeding the venerable Fernão Lopes, who had held that title since the days of John I. From his two principal works, the *Crónica da Tomada de Ceuta* and the *Crónica da Guiné*, it is clear that he held a position of confidence in the household of Henry the Navigator as well. In fact, it appears he knew several of the early explorers personally, which gives his accounts unparalleled insight. Both chronicles were officially commissioned by Afonso V during the 1450s, but it is possible that Azurara drew from earlier accounts, compiled during the heyday of Henry's explorations in the 1440s. While invaluable,

Azurara's writings have an unfortunate tendency to see the exploration of the northwest African coast as a crusade. When in later years economic objectives gradually replaced religious motivations, and traders began to succeed knights, he seems to have lost interest in the process, possibly explaining why he never wrote the promised completion of his account. An annotated English translation of the *Crónica da Guiné* was published by the Hakluyt Society (London) in 1896 (Vol.96) and 1898 (Vol.100).

JOÃO DE BARROS

Born in 1496, João de Barros was raised at the court of King Manuel, an experience that guaranteed him an excellent education. Growing up during a period of Asian euphoria, Barros decided to write an account of Portugal's overseas exploits at an early age, although he didn't get to do so until much later in life. He was first appointed to a posting at the fortress of El Mina; a subsequent posting in Brazil was cut short because of a shipwreck. From the early 1530s Barros resided in Lisbon, where he had been appointed Factor of the Casa da India—a job which gave him responsibility over the annual fleets to India. In that position Barros had access to all kinds of records which provided the source material for his work. The first volume of his acclaimed *Décadas da Ásia* appeared in 1552. Three more volumes followed over the next eighteen years. Barros died in Lisbon in 1570. Though the *Décadas* is unquestionably one of the most interesting and readable accounts of the early contacts between Europeans, Africans and Asians, it has yet to be translated into English.

ALVISE DA CADAMOSTO

A Venetian merchant, Cadamosto (1432–1488) wrote one of the most interesting eyewitness accounts of the early period of African exploration. After obtaining permission from Prince Henry and investing in the trade, Cadamosto visited West Africa on two occasions, reaching as far as today's Bissau, and possibly sighting the Cape Verde Islands on his second trip. On his return to Venice he wrote an account of his adventures, which became quite popular throughout Europe. Cadamosto included an appendix, covering the last voyage commissioned by Prince Henry—a voyage which went as far as Sierra

Leone. An English translation of Cadamosto's highly original work was published by the Hakluyt Society (London) in 1938 (Series II, Vol.80).

LUÍS DE CAMÕES

Although Luís de Camões will forever be known as the author of Portugal's national epic *Os Lusiades* (The Lusiads), not a great deal is known about the man and his life. It is not certain when or where he was born, aside from the fact that it must have been in the mid-1520s. During his youth he studied at the University of Coimbra, but little is known about his activities prior to his leaving for India in 1553. His sixteen years in the Orient are better documented. Camões apparently fought bravely in several military expeditions along the Malabar coast and in the Red Sea. In 1556 he went further east and spent two years in Macao shortly after its establishment. Then he decided to head back to Lisbon, but the trip home turned into a veritable Odyssey, delayed by shipwreck, imprisonment, and poverty. Camões didn't make it back to Lisbon until 1570. Two years later *Os Lusiades* was published. While the work was well received and popular, legend has it that Camões spent his final years in poverty. Though no longer universally accepted, it is clear that his final years were marked by problems. Camões died in 1580, possibly of the plague. Portugal lost its greatest poet at the same time as it lost its independence to Spain.

DIOGO CÃO

Diogo Cão is one of the great mystery figures of the Portuguese explorations: a man about whom hardly anything is known despite of the magnitude of his achievements. Presumably a member of the king's household, Cão was appointed to lead the first major exploratory voyage of John II's reign in 1481 or 1482. The trip brought him as far as the Zaire river estuary and Cape St. Maria at 13 degrees S (near Benguela in today's Angola). Honored and rewarded by the king, Cão was asked to head a second voyage which took him as far as Cape Cross in today's Namibia. Some historians believe Cão completed his exploration in three voyages, but of that there is no certainty. Cão may have returned to Lisbon in 1486, as Barros implies, or he may have died on the return of his last voyage, a possibility supported by the fact that there are no further references to him in the records.

BARTOLOMEU DIAS

Though Bartolomeu Dias is widely known as the conqueror of the Cape of Good Hope, not a great deal is known about his life. There are no references to the place or year of his birth. Prior to his epochal voyage he was a squire in the household of John II, which must have brought him in contact with people like Diogo Cão and some of his predecessors. Although Dias' achievement opened the door to the sea route to India, it appears that he was not greatly rewarded by John II. Nonetheless, Dias continued to serve the interests of the crown, possibly captaining a ship in the mouth of the Tagus during the early 1490s, and serving as tax collector at El Mina between 1494 and 1496. He seems to have been involved in the preparations for Vasco da Gama's voyage, though it is not clear to what extent. During Manuel's reign he was granted captaincy of a ship on the second fleet to India. Unfortunately the vessel sank along with three others during a South Atlantic storm. Bartolomeu Dias and all aboard vanished without a trace.

GIL EANES

Of Gil Eanes, along with the other navigators of the early voyages along the West African coast, little is known aside from their navigational achievements. Eanes, of course, is rightly known for the passing of Cape Bojador in 1434, a feat that is generally considered to mark the onset of the explorations. Though relatively short in distance, the voyage was a milestone. Bojador may have been no more than a small feature on the map, but in the mind of early navigators it had stood as a formidable obstacle for many years. Eanes is also known to have captained the next voyage south along with Gonçalves Baldaia, a trip that went as far as Angra dos Ruivos and revealed proof of human habitation. According to Azurara, Eanes went to Africa twice more—once on a slave raiding trip to Arguim and a final time on a trip that took him as far as Cape Verde. Like most of his colleagues, Eanes was a squire to Prince Henry, and later a knight. None of these people were schooled or raised as sailors or navigators, but what they achieved at sea was as impressive and courageous as the first explorations of the space age.

HENRY THE NAVIGATOR

Known in Portugal as the Infante Dom Henrique, Prince Henry was born in Porto on 4 March 1394, the third surviving son of John I and Philippa of Lancaster. Generally and rightly considered to be the initiator of the Portuguese expansion, a good many books have been written about him. It is understandable that sixteenth-century Portuguese historians, in an effort to interpret their country's dramatic changes, examined his life and contributions, but Henry also caught the fancy of Victorian historians, accounting for numerous nineteenth-century books and articles. While these works are generally positive—some bordering on reverence—recent accounts provide more objective assessments. They reveal a more ambiguous figure, part feudal lord and part businessman, with few of the romantic qualities bestowed on him by earlier writers. Even so, there is little doubt that through his sponsorship, patience and perseverance, Henry was the key to Portugal's first overseas excursions.

JOHN II

Prince John (1455–1495), the oldest son of Afonso V and Queen Isabel and thus the grandnephew of Henry the Navigator, continued the work initiated by his illustrious great-uncle. John was knighted by his father after the Portuguese conquest of Arzila (1471), and from then on began to play a greater role in the country's political affairs. In 1474 his father put him in charge of Portugal's overseas policy. Although the internal political situation, along with the war with Castile, prevented John from dispatching new voyages, he secured Portugal's rights to the African coast south of the Canary Islands. In 1481 John ascended the throne as Portugal's thirteenth king. Shortly thereafter, he ordered the construction of a fortress in today's Ghana as well as a new voyage of exploration, this time south of the equator. Aside from sponsoring the search for passage around Africa to the Indies, John never lost sight of the need for additional support and information. He implemented a broad African policy, establishing additional bases and alliances and sending people overland to India and East Africa to collect information. Once Bartolomeu Dias had rounded the Cape of Good Hope, John probably dispatched additional voyages to seek a safe South Atlantic passage. Finally, when Columbus returned with news of land in the western Atlantic, John masterminded the division of the world between Portugal and Spain. Like Bartolomeu Dias, he would never lay eyes on the Indies, but he, more than anyone else, made the voyages to the East possible.

MANUEL I

Manuel I (1469–1521), fourteenth king of Portugal, presided over the country's golden age of exploration, dispatching the voyages of Vasco da Gama, Pedro Cabral, Gaspar Corte-Real, and Afonso de Albuquerque. Although he reached the throne in a somewhat unconventional manner, Manuel was convinced he was a key part of some divine design, a belief that led to excessive religious zeal and a number of missionary enterprises in Portugal's overseas possessions. He also initiated the persecution of the Jews in Portugal, which led to their expulsion from the country in 1497–1498. During his reign, Portugal acquired great wealth from the trade with and in Asia, allowing for the construction of magnificent buildings like the Jeronimos monastery outside Lisbon. It also permitted Manuel to develop his court into a center of arts and sciences which was the envy of all Europe.

DUARTE PACHECO PEREIRA

Though not much discussed in this book, Duarte Pacheco Pereira is one of the great names in the Portuguese expansion. Born in the middle of the fifteenth century, he first served the court of John II and in time became one of his advisors, a function that probably put him face-to-face with Columbus when the Genoan petitioned the King for support. Pereira made several voyages himself, including a trip to El Mina in the early 1480s and one to central Africa later in the decade, where he was picked up by Bartolomeu Dias on his return from the Cape. Pereira would have been likely to be a South Atlantic explorer in the years prior to Vasco da Gama's voyage. In fact, in some of his writing he hints at a sighting of Brazil well before its "official" discovery in 1500. Pereira went to India in 1503 with Afonso de Albuquerque and showed his mettle as soldier and strategist during the siege of Cochin, where he commanded the Portuguese contingent. But his principle claim to fame is his book *Esmeraldo do Situ Orbis*—the first *roteiro* (rutter) to describe the coasts between Portugal and India, with information on coastal peoples, their ways of life, and their commerce thrown in for good measure. Though written early in the sixteenth century, it is still relevant along some stretches of the coast and, in fact, exceeds modern sources in terms of detail. The book was published in English by the Hakluyt Society in 1937. A true figure of the renaissance—sailor, scientist and soldier—Pereira died in 1530.

FERNÃO MENDES PINTO

Though his *Peregrinição* (Travels) ranks as one of the great autobiographical accounts of the sixteenth century, not a great deal is known about Fernão Mendes Pinto. In fact, his book is a relatively poor source of biographical material because it is difficult to separate fact from fiction. More authoritative information comes from other sources, especially the Jesuits with whom Pinto was affiliated for some time. It is they who confirm his activities in Japan, lending credence to much of what he has to say about the country. For much of what happened earlier in his life, Pinto's book is the main source. It is there that Pinto tells us he was born in Montemor-o-Velho, a small town halfway between Coimbra and the coast in central Portugal, and how he spent the first twenty-five years of his life prior to leaving for the Indies in 1537. There is little doubt he spent the next two decades traveling throughout the East, alternating roles as trader, soldier, adventurer, and, upon occasion, ambassador. He returned to Lisbon in September 1558 where, sometime between 1569 and 1578, he wrote the *Travels*. The book wouldn't be published until thirty years after Pinto's death in 1583. Though it has suffered through many poor translations and adaptions, a brilliant English translation was completed by Rebecca Catz and published by the University of Chicago Press in 1989.

ÁLVARO VELHO

It is difficult to find anything at all about Álvaro Velho, aside from the fact that he was one of the approximately 150 men that accompanied Vasco da Gama on the first voyage to India. There isn't even certainty that he wrote the one surviving eyewitness account attributed to him. His claim to authorship is based largely on a process of elimination—for instance, it is known that the author served on the *São Rafael* and that he mentions the names of others, who can obviously be eliminated from the list of possible authors. Given its style, it is clear that the notes were kept by someone with a decent education. That certainly would rule out a good many sailors and soldiers in the fleet, most of whom wouldn't have been literate. The account ends off the West African coast, raising questions as to whether its author actually survived the voyage. We'll never know. There are accounts of one Velho having been encountered in Guinea in subsequent years, but whether that is the same person is not at all certain. An English translation of Velho's account was published by the Hakluyt Society (Series I Vol. 99) on the occasion of the fourth centenary of the voyage of Vasco da Gama in 1898.

A Chronology Of The Portuguese Expansion

1385	Accession of King John I, founder of the Aviz dynasty.
1394	Birth in Oporto of Henry the Navigator
1415	The conquest of Ceuta, generally regarded as the curtain-raiser to the Portuguese expansion.
1419	Discovery of Porto Santo by João Gonçalves Zarco and Tristão Vaz, followed a year later by that of Madeira.
1424	Fernando de Castro is sent to the Canary Islands. Castilian opposition thwarts the Portuguese plan to establish a base.
1425	Colonization of Madeira.
1427	Diogo de Silves discovers the Azores.
1433	Prince Edward is crowned king of Portugal, following the death of John I.
1434	Gil Eanes rounds Cape Bojador.
1435	Gil Eanes and Afonso Gonçalves Baldaia sail beyond Bojador and discover signs of human habitation at Angra dos Ruivos in today's Western Sahara.
1436	Afonso Gonçalves Baldaia reaches the Rio de Ouro. Some of his men encounter natives but fail to capture any.
1437	The Portuguese campaign to conquer Tangier is a total failure.
1438	Death of King Edward. His brother Pedro becomes regent.
1441	Antão Gonçalves captures the first people in northwest Africa and brings them to Portugal.
	Nuno Tristão sails as far as Cabo Branco (Cap Blanc) in today's Mauretania.
1443	Dom Pedro grants his brother Henry the exclusive right to navigate the waters south of Cape Bojador.
	Nuno Tristão discovers the islands of Tider and Arguin off the Mauretanian coast.
1444	Nuno Tristão reaches the Senegal River.
	Dias Dinis sights Cape Verde, continental Africa's westernmost point.

1445	Establishment of a trading post on Arguin Island. It is the first European base in Africa.
1452	Diogo de Teive discovers the islands of Flores and Corvo of the Azores archipelago.
1453	Azurara writes his *Crónica da Guiné*.
1455	The papal bull *Romanus pontifex* confirms the Portuguese claim to the lands discovered south of the Canary Islands.
	Birth of Prince John, the future King John II.
	Cadamosto leaves on his first voyage to Africa.
c. 1456	Sighting of the Cape Verde Islands by Cadamosto.
1458	Afonso V conquers Alcázar Seguer along the North African coast.
c. 1460	Pero de Sintra discovers Sierra Leone.
1460	Henry the Navigator dies in Sagres, bringing Portugal's African exploration to a temporary halt.
1462	First settlements on the Cape Verde islands.
c.1468	Birth of Vasco da Gama
1469	The Portuguese crown signs a contract with Fernão Gomes to continue the exploration of the West African coast.
	Birth of Manuel, duke of Beja and future king.
1471	King Afonso V captures Arzila. Tangier capitulates.
	João de Santarém and Pêro de Escobar reach the Gold Coast in today's Ghana.
1472	Fernão do Pó sails as far as the Bight of Biafra.
c.1472	The islands of São Tomé and Príncipe are discovered.
c.1474	Rui de Sequeira crosses the equator and sails as far as Cape Santa Catherina (Gabon).
1474	Prince John assumes control of Portugal's African interests.
1475	Columbus arrives in Lisbon, and settles in the Genoese community.
1476	Afonso V claims the throne of Castile but is defeated by Ferdinand of Aragon.
1479	The Treaty of Alcâçovas settles the dispute between Portugal and Castile and reaffirms Portuguese control over the lands discovered south of the Canary Islands.
c.1480	Portuguese envoys reach Mali.

1481   Death of Afonso V. John II ascends the throne.

1482   The fortress of São Jorge is constructed at El Mina.

c.1482   First voyage of Diogo Cão reaches the Zaire River and continues as far today's Benguela.

c.1483   Columbus's proposal to sail west in search of the East is rejected by John II's council.

c.1485   Second voyage of Diogo Cão. This time he reaches Cape Cross, Namibia. In the course of two voyages Cão added nearly fifteen-hundred miles to the African map.

1486   João Afonso de Aveira reaches the kingdom of Benin.

1487   Pêro da Covilhã and Afonso Paiva are dispatched to India and Ethiopia. Paiva dies during his travels. Covilhã reaches India, Ethiopia and East Africa over the next several years.

     John II sends a three-vessel fleet headed by Bartolomeu Dias to round the African continent.

1488   Dias rounds the Cape of Good Hope and Cape Agulhas, Africa's southernmost point. He sails as far as the Great Fish river prior to returning to Lisbon.

1491   Rui de Sousa arrives in the kingdom of the Congo. At Ambasse, its capital, the king, queen and many of their subjects are converted to Christianity.

1492   Conquest of Granada. Shortly thereafter Ferdinand and Isabella authorize Columbus's voyage.

1494   The treaty of Tordesillas divides the world into Portuguese and Spanish spheres of interest.

1495   Death of John II. His cousin Manuel ascends the throne.

c.1495   João Fernandes Lavrador and Pêro de Barcelos land on Greenland.

1497   Departure of Vasco da Gama. His fleet reaches India in May of the following year.

1500   Pedro Álvares Cabral steps ashore in Brazil during the outbound leg of the second voyage to India.

     Gaspar Corte Real reaches Terra Nova (Newfoundland).

     Portuguese navigators sight Madagascar.

1502   Vasco da Gama departs on his second voyage to India.

1503   Trading factories are established in Brazil.

Portuguese navigators reach the Seychelles.

1505   Francisco de Almeida is appointed first viceroy of the Estate of India and leaves Lisbon aboard a heavily armed fleet.

The Portuguese construct fortresses in Kilwa and Sofala, East Africa.

1506   Lourenço de Almeida arrives in Ceylon.

1509   Diogo Lopes de Sequeira reaches Sumatra and Malacca.

1510   Afonso de Albuquerque captures Goa.

c.1510 Fernão Mendes Pinto is born in Montemor-o-Velho, Portugal.

1511   Afonso de Albuquerque captures Malacca.

Duarte Fernandes is the first European to visit Siam.

1512   Rui Nunes reaches the kingdom of Pegu in today's Burma.

Francisco Serrão lands in the Moluccas.

The Portuguese establish a factory in Calicut.

1513   Jorge Álvares leads the first Portuguese trade mission to China.

1514   A Portuguese embassy reaches the court of the shah of Persia.

António Fernandes leaves for Central Africa, reaching present-day Zimbabwe and the then kingdom of Monomotapa.

1515   The first Portuguese missionaries arrive in the kingdom of Benin, West Africa.

Afonso de Albuquerque captures Hormuz.

c.1515 The Portuguese arrive in Timor

1516   Tomé Pires, first Portuguese ambassador to China, leaves Goa for Canton and Peking.

1519   Fernão de Magalhães [Ferdinand Magellan], sailing for the Spanish crown, leaves on what became the first circum-navigation of the world.

1520   A Portuguese embassy headed by Rodrigo de Lima reaches the court of the Negus (Prester John) in Ethiopia.

1521   Death of Manuel. His son ascends the throne as John III.

1524   Vasco da Gama leaves for India on his third and final voyage. He dies in Cochin on Christmas Eve of the same year.

1537	The Portuguese obtain a new Indian base in Diu.
	Fernão Mendes Pinto sails for India.
1543	Three Portuguese arrive in Tanegashima, Japan.
1549	Francis Xavier arrives in Japan. He dies two years later off the Chinese coast.
1552	João de Barros publishes the first volume of his *Décadas*.
1557	The Portuguese obtain the right to use Macao, the first European base in China.
	John III dies. Sebastian becomes the new king.
1559	The Portuguese send an embassy into Angola.
1571	The Portuguese obtain the right to use Nagasaki.
1575	Oda Nobunaga defeats his opponents at the battle of Nagashino and consolidates his grip on all of Japan.
1578	The Portuguese king Sebastian dies at Alcázar Quibir, Morocco. Because he left no heir, the crowns of Spain and Portugal are unified from 1580 to 1640.
1593	The Portuguese begin to construct Fort Jesus, Mombasa.
1605	The Dutch capture Portuguese bases in the Moluccas.
1614	The *Peregrinação* (*Travels*) of Fernão Mendes Pinto are finally published, more than thirty years after its author's death in 1583.
1622	The Portuguese lose their fortress in Hormuz.
1637	A Dutch squadron captures the Portuguese base and fortress at El Mina.
1638	A group of Japanese peasants, many of them Christian, rebel against the lord of Shimabara.
1640	The Portuguese are expelled from Japan.
1641	Malacca is captured by the Dutch.
1650	The Portuguese are evicted from the Persian Gulf.
1652	The Portuguese are defeated in Zanzibar.
1655	The Portuguese forces in Mombasa capitulate.
1658	The Portuguese lose Ceylon.
1663	The Dutch capture several Portuguese settlements on India's Malabar Coast.

Selected References

Adam, Ahmat. *Portuguese Words in the Malay Language*. International Seminar on Silk Roads. Malacca, Malaysia, 1991.

Albuquerque, Luís de. *Instruments of Navigation*. Lisbon: National Commission for the Commemoration of the Portuguese Discoveries, 1988.

Álvares, Francisco. *The Prester John of the Indies. A True Relation of the Lands of the Prester John*. Hakluyt Society Publications, 2d ser., vols. 114 and 115, London, 1961.

Arhin, Kwame, ed. *The Cape Coast and Elmina Handbook*. Legon: University of Ghana, 1995.

Axelson, Eric. *South-East Africa, 1488–1530*. London and New York: Longmans, Green & Co., 1940.

———. *Congo to Cape: Early Portuguese Explorers*. New York: Harper & Row, 1973.

Azurara, Gomes Eanes de. *Crónica do Descobrimento e Conquista da Guiné*. Hakluyt Society Publications, 1st ser, vol. 95 and vol. 100. London, 1896 and 1898.

Badriyay Haji Salleh. *Melaka's Cosmopolitan Society During the Melaka Sultanate*. International Seminar on Silk Roads. Malacca, Malaysia, 1991.

Barbosa, Duarte. *The Book of Duarte Barbosa: An Account of the Countries Bordering on the Indian Ocean and their Inhabitants*. Hakluyt Society Publications, 2d ser., vols. 44 and 49. London 1921.

Barraclough, Geoffrey, ed. *The Times Atlas of World History*. New York: Hammond, 1984.

Barros, João de. *Décadas da Ásia, Volumes i–iv*. Lisbon: Livraria Sá da Costa, 1946.

Bell, Christopher. *Portugal and the Quest for the Indies*. New York: Barnes & Noble, 1974.

Bender, Gerald R.. *Angola under the Portuguese*. Berkeley and Los Angeles: University of California Press, 1978.

Berthon, Simon, and Andrew Robinson. *The Shape of the World*. Chicago: Rand McNally, 1991.

Blake, John W., ed. *Europeans in West Africa, 1450–1560*. Hakluyt Society Publications, 2d ser., vols. 86 and 87. London, 1942.

Blussé, Leonard, and Femme Gaastra, eds. *Companies and Trade*. Leiden, the Netherlands: Leiden University Press, 1981.

Boorstin, Daniel J. *The Discoverers*. New York: Vintage Books, 1985.

Bouvier, Nicolas. *The Japanese Chronicles*. San Francisco: Mercury House, 1992.

Boxer, Charles R.. *Race Relations in the Portuguese Colonial Empire, 1415–1825*. Oxford: Clarendon Press, 1963.

———. *The Christian Century in Japan, 1549–1650*. Berkeley and Los Angeles: University of California Press, 1967.

———. *Fidalgos in the Far East, 1550-1770*. Oxford: Oxford University Press, 1968.

———. *The Portuguese Seaborne Empire: 1415–1825*. London: Hutchinson and Co., 1969.

———. *João de Barros—Portuguese Humanist and Historian of Asia*. New Delhi: Concept Publishing Company, 1981.

———. *The Great Ship from Amacon—Annals of Macau and the Old Japan Trade, 1550–1640*. Lisbon: Centro de Estudos Históricos Ultramarinos, 1988.

———. ed. *The Tragic History of the Sea, 1589–1622*. Hakluyt Society Publications, 2d ser., vol. 132. London, 1968.

Broeze, Frank, ed. *Brides of the Sea—Port Cities of Asia from the 16th–20th Centuries*. Honolulu: University of Hawaii Press, 1989.

Cadamosto, Alvise da. *Voyages*. Hakluyt Society Publications, 2d ser., vol. 80. London, 1938.

Camões, Luís Vaz de. *Os Lusiades (The Lusiads)*. English translation by William C. Atkinson. London: Penguin Books, 1952.

Catz, Rebecca D. ed. *The Travels of Mendes Pinto*. Chicago: The University of Chicago Press, 1989.

Catz, Rebecca. "Who Discovered Japan?" *Portuguese Studies Review* 3, no. 1 1993.

Cooper, Michael S. J. Ed. *They Came to Japan—An Anthology of European Reports on Japan, 1543–1640*. London: Thames and Hudson, 1963.

Correia-Afonso, John. *Jesuit Letters and Indian History: 1542–1773*. Bombay: Oxford University Press, 1969.

Correia-Afonso, John, ed. *Indo-Portuguese History: Sources and Problems*. Bombay: Oxford University Press, 1981.

Council of Europe. *Portugal: A Pioneer of the North–South Dialogue*. Lisbon: Imprensa Nacional–Casa Da Moeda, 1988.

Crone, Gerald R. ed. *The Voyages of Cadamosto and Other Documents* on *Western Africa in the Second Half of the Fifteenth Century.* Hakluyt Society Publications, 2d ser., vol. 80. London, 1937.

Daehnhardt, Rainer. *The Bewitched Gun: The Introduction of Firearms in the Far East by the Portuguese.* Lisbon: Texto Editora, 1994.

Fonseca, Luís Adão da. "Bartolomeu Dias and the Origins of Modernity," in *Bartolomeu Dias,* 500th Anniversary Commemoration in Durban. Porto: Funadação Eng. António de Almeida, 1990.

Davidson, Basil. *African Kingdoms.* Alexandria, Virginia: Time-Life Books, 1978.

D'Avila Lourido, Rui, *The Maritime Route Macau–Manila in the 16–17th century.* Regional Conference on the Maritime Silk Trade. Manila, February 1990.

Diffie, Bailey W., and George Winius. *Foundations of the Portuguese Empire 1415–1580.* Minneapolis: University of Minnesota Press, 1977.

Disney, A. R.. *Twilight of the Pepper Empire—Portuguese Trade in Southwest India in the Early Seventeenth Century.* Cambridge: Harvard University Press, 1978.

Duncan, B.. *Atlantic Islands—Madeira, the Azores and the Cape Verde Islands in Seventeenth Century Commerce and Navigation.* Chicago: University of Chicago Press, 1972.

Fundação Calouste Gulbenkian. *Portugal e a Tailândia.* Lisbon: Gulbenkian Foundation, 1988.

Furber, Holden. *Rival Empires of Trade in the Orient, 1600 –1800.* Minneapolis, University of Minnesota Press, 1986.

Galvão, António, *Discoveries of the World.* Hakluyt Society Publications, London, 1863.

Garcia, José Manuel. *Sagres.* Vila do Bispo: Vila Do Bispo Municipal Council, 1990.

———. *Portugal and the Discoveries.* Lisbon: Commission of Portugal for the Seville Universal Exhibition, 1992.

———. *Europa Japão—Um Diálogo Civilizacional no Século XVI.* Lisbon: Cômissâo Nacional para as Comemoracões dos Descobrimentos Portugueses (CNCDP), 1993.

———. *Portugal and the Division of the World.* Lisbon: Portuguese State Mint, 1994.

Graham, J. Erskine. *Cape Coast in History.* Cape Coast: Anglican Printing Press (1994).

Greenlee, William Brooks. *The Voyage of Pedro Álvares Cabral to Brazil and India.* Hakluyt Society Publications, London, 1938.

Guedes, Max Justo, and Gerald Lombardi eds. *Portugal–Brazil: The Age of Atlantic Discoveries*. Lisbon: Bertrand Editora, 1990.

Guerreiro, Inácio. *Effects of the Voyages to the Extreme East and Indian Ocean in the European Cartography of the 14th and 15th Centuries*. International Seminar on Silk Roads. Malacca, Malaysia, 1991.

Hale, John R., *Renaissance Exploration*. New York: W. W. Norton & Company, 1958.

———. *Age of Exploration*. Amsterdam: Time-Life Books, 1966.

Hart, Henry H. *Sea Road to the Indies*. New York: Macmillan , 1950.

Hourani, George F.. *Arab Seafaring in the Indian Ocean in Ancient and Early Medieval Times*. New York: Octagon Books, 1975.

Hyma, Albert. *A History of the Dutch in the Far East*. Ann Arbor: George Wahr, 1953.

Jackson, Kenneth David, *A Hidden Presence—500 years of Portuguese Culture in India and Sri Lanka*. Macao: Fundação Macau, 1995.

Jesus, C.A. Montalto de. *Historic Macau*. Hong Kong: Oxford University Press, 1984.

Kagoshima Historical Material Preservation Center. *Tradition of Firearms: 450 years*. Kagoshima: Reimei-kan, 1993

Kirkman, James. *Gedi*. Nairobi: National Museums of Kenya, 1975.

Kirkman, James. *Fort Jesus*. Mombasa: National Museums of Kenya, 1981.

Linschoten, J. H. *The Voyage of Jan Huyghen van Linschoten to the East Indies*. Hakluyt Society Publications, 1st ser., vols. 70 and 71. London, 1885.

Martin, Esmond B., and Martin, Chryssee. P. *Cargoes of the East—The Ports, Trade and Culture of the Arabian Seas and Western Indian Ocean*. London: Elm Tree Books, 1969.

Miller, Russell. *The East Indiamen*. Alexandria, Virginia: Time-Life Books, 1981.

Nanpo Bunshi. *Teppo Ki*. Tanegashima Development Center.

Newby, Eric. *The World Atlas of Exploration*. New York: Crescent Books, 1985.

Parry, J. H. *The Age of Reconnaissance*. London: Weidenfeld and Nicholson, 1963.

———. *The Discovery of the Sea*. New York: Dial Press, 1974.

Penrose, B. *Travel and Discovery in the Renaissance*. Cambridge: Harvard University Press, 1952.

Pereira, Duarte Pacheco. *Esmeralda do Situ Orbis*. Hakluyt Society Publications, ser 2d., vol. 79. London, 1937.

Pereira, Luís Felipe. *Ilha de Moçambique, Ponto de Encontro de*

Civilizações. Maputo: Comissário-geral de Moçambique na Exposição Universal de Sevilha, 1992.

Pinto, Paulo Jorge Sousa. "Melaka, Johor and Aceh: A bird's eye view over a Portuguese-Malay Triangular Balance (1575–1619)." *Arquivos de Centro Cultural Calouste Gulbenkian*, Vol. 35, pp. 109-131 (1996).

Pires, Tomé. *The Suma Oriental of Tomé Pires*. Hakluyt Society Publications, 2d ser., vol. 89. London, 1944.

Rajagopalan, S.. *Old Goa*. New Delhi: Archaeological Survey of India, 1994.

Rodrigues, Avelino, Leong Ka Tai and Gonçalo César de Sâ. *Tanegashima, the Island of the Portuguese Gun*. Macau: Instituto Cultural de Macau, 1988.

Rogers, Francis M. *The Travels of Dom Pedro of Portugal*. Cambridge: Harvard University Press, 1961.

Russell-Wood, A.J.R. *A World on the Move—The Portuguese in Africa, Asia and America, 1415–1808*. Manchester: Carcanet Press, 1992.

Scammell, G. V.. *The World Encompassed—the first European Maritime Empires: c. 800–1650*. Berkeley and Los Angeles: University of California Press, 1981.

Soledade, Arnalodo. *Sines–Terra de Vasco da Gama*. Alcácer de Sal: Francisco Martins d'Almeida, 1990.

Souza, Teotonio, ed. *Indo-Portuguese History: Old Issues—New Questions*. New Delhi: Concept Publishing Co., 1985.

Strandes, Justus. *The Portuguese Period in East Africa*. Nairobi: Kenya Literature Bureau, 1989.

Subrahmanjan, Sanjay. *The Career and Legend of Vasco da Gama*. Cambridge: Cambridge University Press, 1997.

Tadashi, Kikuoka, "Teppo-ki (The Chronicle of the Arquebus)." *The East*, 47–50.

Taylor, L.C., ed. *Luis de Camões—Epic & Lyic*. Manchester: Carcanet Press, 1990.

Teague, Michael. *In the Wake of the Portuguese Navigators*. Manchester: Carcanet Press, 1988.

Tooley, R. V.. *Maps and Map Makers*. New York: Dorset Press, 1987.

Velho, Álvaro, Attributed. *A Journal of the First Voyage of Vasco da Gama, 1497–1499*. Hakluyt Society Publications, 1st ser., vol. 99. London, 1898.

Videira Pires, Benjamin. "Mutual Influences between Portugal and China," *Review of Culture*, (1988) 76–83.

Villiers, Alan. *Monsoon Seas—The Story of the Indian Ocean*. New York: McGraw-Hill 1947.

———. *Sons of Sinbad*. New York: Charles Scribner's Sons, 1939.

Williams, J.E.D. *From Sails to Satellites—The Origin and Development of Navigational Science*. Oxford: Oxford University Press, 1992.

Yahaya Abu Bakar. *Foreign Documents and the Description of Melaka between A.D. 1505–1511*. International Seminar on Silk Roads. Malacca, Malaysia, 1991.

Yuuki, Diego R. *The Way of Xavier*. Nagasaki: Nagasaki Photo Service Co., 1988

Index

About the Author

Luc Cuyvers is a writer, photographer, and filmmaker who specializes in ocean issues. He has developed several international television co-productions on the oceans, most recently 'Into the Rising Sun,' which he also directed. Aside from his television work, Cuyvers has written six books on marine issues. He holds a doctorate in marine studies from the University of Delaware, and divides his time between his hometown of Antwerp, Belgium, and Annapolis, Maryland.